Kim Mooney is a teacher and writer. She holds an undergraduate degree in mathematics and a master's degree in leadership. Her career has been an eclectic one, moving between teaching and hospital administration and back to teaching. She retired in 2018 after fifteen years of teaching at Royal Roads University in Victoria, BC. With Kim's first published story in 1970 came a prize—a typewriter. A few short stories and a series of poems were written on that machine and then set aside in a drawer. This is Kim's first published book. She and her husband, Chad, divide their time between Vancouver and the Southern Gulf Islands.

To Pat, for your courage.

To Mom and Dad, for your fierce love.

To Chad, for being my champion.

Kim Mooney

HIDDEN DAUGHTER –
SECRET SISTER

A Story of Adoption

AUSTIN MACAULEY PUBLISHERS™

LONDON · CAMBRIDGE · NEW YORK · SHARJAH

Ordering Information:
Quantity sales: special discounts are available on quantity purchases by corporations, associations, and others. For details, contact the publisher at the address below.

Publisher's Cataloging-in-Publication data
Mooney, Kim
Hidden Daughter – Secret Sister

ISBN 9781645369837 (Paperback)
ISBN 9781645369844 (Hardback)
ISBN 9781645369868 (ePub e-book)

Library of Congress Control Number: 2020909718

www.austinmacauley.com/us

First Published (2020)
Austin Macauley Publishers LLC
40 Wall Street, 28th Floor
New York, NY 10005
USA

mail-usa@austinmacauley.com
+1 (646) 5125767

When you start to write a book, you sit alone and stare at your computer, waiting for your fingers to begin the tapping required to make the words appear. Some days that tactic works and sometimes it doesn't. That is when people begin to give you support. Each one brings a gift and sets it down in front of you. Each time this happens, the writing moves forward. Thank you for believing in me, trusting that I would tell my story with respect and grace. Without your encouragement, I would still be sitting, staring at the keys. Waiting.

Jennifer Gunning for being, without question, my first editor. Your enthusiasm and kind words helped me focus.

Judy Kern, my intrepid editor! You pushed me to write clearly, to tell the whole story with clarity. No whining!

Christina Baldwin and my peer spirit circle—you encouraged the baby bird to fly!

My two friends (you know who you are!) from Mums and Tots—your trust opened the door to here.

Paul, Cheryl, Carla, John, and James—thank you for you sharing your stories with openness and enthusiasm, trusting me to use your words carefully.

Alan Morinis, Mel McLeod, Julie Holder, Sheila Kiscaden, and Barb Stoddard for your thoughtful comments and belief that I would succeed.

Kim, Robin, and Miji Campbell for welcoming me as your sister and for sharing your stories.

Shawna and Matthew—my children. You are woven into the fabric of my soul and I am a better person because of you. No story about me is complete without you. You are kind and generous people. I love you both with all my heart.

Chad, for your clarity when I was struggling, for your patience when I was hiding, for your love that shines through everything.

To each of you, I will be forever grateful.

And finally, to the women and men who go about their daily lives, living with the questions of their birth, and still live their lives the best way they can.

"Stories that instruct, renew, and heal provide a vital nourishment to the psyche that cannot be obtained in any other way.

Stories reveal over and over again the precious and peculiar knack that humans have for triumph over travail. They provide all the vital instructions we need to live a useful, necessary, and unbounded life – a life of meaning, a life worth remembering."

Clarrisa Pinkola Estes

2016 – Prologue

Writing a story about an important event in your life seems like it should be an easy task. All you need to do is dig into the depths of your memory bank and pull out the pieces that make the story interesting and rich—something that everyone will want to read. Except, it isn't that easy. The memories merge or bounce off one another, confusing what really happened, what might have happened, and what you want to have happened. And there is never just one story. There are multiple versions, layers, and points of view. To tell a story with just the facts leaves most of the story untold. Telling the whole story requires looking under rocks, into crevasses, and searching for why the story seemed so important to tell in the first place. Facts are okay but if that's all there is, the magic is missed because the whole messy story—well it's so much more. To write this story, with all the messiness, complexity, pain, and acceptance that comes with it, has been my challenge.

So, how does one do that? By opening the windows and blowing out the cobwebs. By exploring the impact that secrets can have on the people who keep them. There is joy and sadness in the story. There are feelings of shame, rejection and abandonment, but also understanding, acceptance and forgiveness.

Writing this story has meant taking a risk, something I have never been good at doing. This is my story of being adopted and how my life unfolded because I was adopted.

1982 – The Spark

There I was on a Tuesday morning, sitting with a group of young mothers at a Mums and Tots group at the local United Church in Richmond, British Columbia. I wasn't normally much of a joiner, but I was desperate for a few minutes of adult conversation. It was a chance to wash away the stickiness of breakfast and talk to someone, anyone, over the age of three or four.

One of the women in the group commented to the mother on my right that her little girl must look like her dad because she certainly didn't look like her mum. A moment passed before the little girl's mother quietly replied that her daughter was adopted. The statement was received and everyone moved on—except me and the woman on my left. For whatever reason, I turned to the adoptive mother and said, "I'm adopted." This was not a fact I generally shared.

The woman on my left then leaned in and said softly, "I gave my daughter away." Now what were the odds of that! For a moment, there was silence among the three of us. A fragile silence enveloped us. We had each retreated into our own memories. From that point on, it was as if there were no one else in the room as we began to tell one another our stories.

The adoptive mother was Anne. She spoke about her deep fear that her daughter's birth mother would come knocking on the door, explaining that she had made a mistake and wanted her daughter back. She also spoke about the shame of not being able to bear her own child. She came from a large family and all her siblings were having babies. It should have been as easy for her as it had been for her sisters. But it seemed that she was unable to have her own child. Her only chance to have a family was to adopt. She said that her blonde, blue-eyed daughter was a gift from God.

Leah, the one who had given up her child confessed to living with the guilt, shame, and anguish of having done that. She had grown up in a small, poor, Catholic community in Quebec where everyone knew everyone else's business and unexpected, unwanted pregnancies were not uncommon, since using any form of birth control was forbidden by the Church. Pregnant at sixteen years old, Leah became the latest statistic, and she hated that it had happened to her. Predictable and shameful, according to the old gossips in town

Having an abortion would have been at least as big a sin as her pregnancy, so she did what other girls in the community had done before her. She had the baby—a girl—and gave her away. After that, she tried to move on, but she knew that her child was living in a neighbouring community with her new family, and, as she told us that morning, she thought about her every day.

Finally, it was my turn. I talked about my childhood fear of being sent back to the orphanage and about how ashamed I was of having been rejected by my birth mother. When I

13

was finished, I touched each of the other two women gently on the arm and said quietly, "I have to leave now," even though it was only about halfway through the play session. Leaving difficult or disturbing situations was my default mode of behavior but, somehow, I knew they would understand.

I swung my three-year-old son up into my arms and headed for my car, squeezing him so tightly that he began to cry. I drove the few blocks home carefully because I was shaking so badly. Tears streamed down my face. My son was jabbering away in his car seat, happy with his own company, while I was engulfed by the childhood memories and feelings of rejection and abandonment that had flooded back in the wake of that morning's conversation.

Chapter One
The Beginning

Life as I have always known it began on December 21, 1952. That was the day my parents came to take me from the orphanage to their home in Vancouver, and, coincidentally, was also their wedding anniversary. I was three months old at the time. They said I was lovely, (even though I was really scrawny, bald, and quite sickly!) that I was their miraculous Christmas gift, and that they fell instantly in love with me. But in the picture I have that was taken that day, I see big brown eyes staring straight ahead. I appear lost. Whenever I look at that photo, I wonder what I might have been feeling. When I asked my parents about how I responded to my new surroundings, they just shrugged and said I seemed content. They were happy so everyone else must have been happy too. The story of my being their Christmas gift became a legend that was repeated over and over in our family.

At the time of my adoption, they already had two children, both boys. Verdun was the child of my mother's previous marriage, and Dan was adopted by my parents four years after Verdun was born and four years before I joined the family. Over the years, I wondered if my brothers were as excited about my Christmas arrival as my parents seemed to be.

My father's name was Reg. I've always thought of him as a kind of renaissance man. He was a voracious reader who loved learning and exploring new ideas. He had been headed for medical school when the Second World War began and his dream came to an abrupt halt. Instead, he joined the Canadian Air Force at nineteen years old and celebrated his twenty-first birthday in a German prison camp, where he survived for two years before managing to escape. He was always reluctant to speak about that time in prison camp, and my brothers and I didn't ask too many questions. The stories he did share were filled with humour and a touch of excitement. I knew these stories were created for our childish minds but they were captivating. The reality of his war remained hidden from us forever. Even when we were adults, he was unwilling to share the cruelties he experienced.

My mother, Phyllis, had lived a thousand lives by the time she met me. Her first husband, whose name was Mac, was killed in World War II. He was twenty-nine years old when he died and my mother was twenty-four. She loved that man with every fiber of her being and often told me the story of the last time she saw him. She had traveled to Montreal from their home in Saskatoon in June,1943 to see him off to England where he would be an instructor for the British Royal Air Force—the RAF. More importantly, she was there to tell him that they were going to have a child. She laughed as she told me how it was improper to say 'pregnant' even to your husband. It seemed that 'being with child' was much more acceptable. They were thrilled and talked of what life would be like when this war ended and they could get on with the life they had planned together. When life returned to 'normal.' He had asked for and received permission to do a fly-by over the apartment building where Mum was staying. She stood on a balcony at the top of the building as he flew over, swung back around, and tipped his wings. As it turned out, that was his final farewell to her. He died on November 7, 1943 during a training flight, five months after he said good-bye to my mother. His plane crashed over the English Channel and his body was never recovered.

My brother, Verd, was born on January 23, 1944. At the time, there were not many options for a widow with a baby. And so, on December 21, 1945, my mother got married again—to that fellow from high school who had always made her laugh. My dad had returned from the war in the spring of 1945 and when he found out that my mother was widowed, he set his sights on winning her heart. My dad loved her very much, had loved her since high school. For her, love and deep devotion would come a little later; meanwhile, respect and friendship provided a solid enough foundation upon which to begin this new chapter in her life.

Both my parents were desperate to have more children. But my mother, after trying five times, was unable to carry another pregnancy to term. So, they decided to adopt and marveled at their good fortune when they brought first Dan and then me into their lives. All three of us kids were embraced as a unit. And, as a family, we would try and prove to the world that nurture could triumph over nature. A conglomerate of odd souls is how I always thought of us.

When my dad returned from the war, he couldn't just take up his old life where he'd left off. His vision had been affected during his time as a prisoner and he was unable to spend the long hours in the lab or library that medical school would have required. The problem later turned out to be a form of post-traumatic stress, but he didn't know it then, and by the time his vision had improved, his dream of going to medical school had vanished. With a new family to support, he tried a few sales jobs but apparently wasn't a very good salesman and was repeatedly let go. I believe that his prison experience affected not only his vision but his ability to concentrate. He did eventually get an office job with a company that was building a hydroelectric dam in northern British Columbia. Unfortunately, that meant being away from his family for long periods of time.

In fact, he had to fly 870 miles from western British Columbia to Vancouver in order to accompany my mother to the orphanage and bring me home. A few days later, right after Christmas, he left again and was gone—except for a few days here and there—for the next 18 months. When he eventually came home for good, it took several months before I'd have anything to do with him. If he touched my food, I wouldn't eat it. If he touched my toys, I wouldn't play with them anymore. If he tried to pick me up, I would cry until he put me down. One of the many family tales is that he handed me a crayon and instead of thanking him, I ate it and then promptly threw it back up onto the floor in front of him. Of course, to me he was at that point a virtual stranger, but, nevertheless, he was devastated. He couldn't understand why I didn't know how much he loved me. To me, that story always seemed to suggest that perhaps I wasn't as grateful to my parents as I should have been, and it always made me feel guilty.

During the 18 months when my dad was away, my mother continued to care for her three children—one of them a very needy baby. Apparently, I was a fussy baby who needed to be fed every two hours, twenty-four hours a day. And to make life just a little more challenging, I had pneumonia twice before I was a year old. I often wondered how my mum managed, but whenever she told the story of my first year and a half, there was a tenderness in her words and a smile in her eyes.

Finally, in 1954, Dad decided to rejoin the air force. By this point his eyes had improved and he would be working in a familiar environment where he felt comfortable. After that, the family was able to stay together, but it also meant that we were constantly criss-crossing Canada from one airbase to another. I attended a different school almost every year until he retired in 1969 when I was in eleventh grade.

At that point, my parents decided to move to the Bahamas, where Dad became a high school teacher. It was an odd decision, given he didn't have a teaching degree. But he had taught at the Officer Staff College when he was in the Air Force, and apparently, the school he applied to decided that his credentials were good enough. He taught mathematics, was promoted to vice principal within a year, and remained at the school for a total of eight years.

By 1969, Verd was working for the Royal Bank of Canada and Dan was in university. I was the only kid left at home, so my parents dragged me with them. I finished my last year of high school in Freeport, Grand Bahama Island

and then returned to Montreal on my own to attend university.

Until we moved to Freeport, I hadn't spent much time with my dad. We had a typical father-daughter relationship. Hellos and goodbyes each day, with very little discussion about what was really going on in each of our lives. He seemed aloof and somewhat unapproachable when I was in my teen years. I could dodge him when I needed to and hang around him when I needed to ask for money or permission to go to dances. Freeport changed all of that. Not only was he teaching at my school, he was teaching me, and we drove to school together every day. It was uncomfortable at first, but slowly we settled into a new rhythm and got to know each other better. We talked about the news of the day or what was happening at school. We related more as equals than as father and daughter.

Interestingly, as I got closer to my dad, my relationship with my mum temporarily deteriorated. We seemed to fight about every little thing, and looking back, I know that I was not very 'nice' to her—more like a seventeen-year-old witch! It was a weird dynamic fueled by jealousy; Mum was left out of the conversations Dad and I were having because she wasn't at school with us. It was an odd and distressing interlude, but by the time I left for university, I had stopped my stroppy behaviour and Mum and I were getting along again.

Nevertheless, my connection to both my parents shifted when I went away to school. Although it took me a while to realize it, the day I left Freeport I began to close the door to my childhood. We still had a great relationship but I stopped needing them. We didn't owe each other anything. Of course, we spent lots of time together over the next many years, but in August 1969, without even realizing it, I decided that from then on, I had to fend for myself. I wasn't always very good at it, but the era of depending on my parents was over. Lots of kids make that kind of move away from their parents as they try to find their feet in the adult world but it felt different to me. It was such a conscious decision. As the plane flew from Freeport to Montreal, I felt a visceral shift in my body. I was on my own. I would have to find my way. It was as if I had been resting in their care for seventeen years and now, that time was over. I didn't always make good decisions and I was scared much of the time but I never looked back.

When they returned to Canada in 1977, Dad went to work for an aircraft manufacturing company, Canadair, located in Montreal, Quebec, and then Kingston, Ontario. He was a manager in the acquisitions department—none of us really knew what that meant or what he did, but he seemed happy. He retired for good in 1985 when he was sixty-four years old. He lived for ten more years and died of cancer when he was seventy-four.

My mother supported my father throughout his many endeavors, always encouraging him to follow his dreams. She trekked with him back and forth across Canada and followed him to the Bahamas. Wherever he went, she went, and she made each move with enthusiasm and good humor. From her I learned to embrace life as it came, to make the best of challenging situations, and to complain as little as possible. Those were good lessons and I took them to heart, but sometimes following in my mother's footsteps stopped me from speaking up for myself. She did whatever she felt was right for my father or her children, and it meant that she rarely did what she wanted to do for herself. If her dreams or aspirations conflicted with Dad's, Dad's dreams always won. When I was a teenager, she went to work in a large department store in Montreal. She loved the work and thrived on her new-found independence. But Dad was already hatching his dream of moving to the Bahamas, even if that meant Mum's leaving her job and giving up the freedom it had provided. I followed her example over and over in the early years of my marriage, abandoning my own ambitions in order to go with my husband wherever his work might take us. It wasn't until many years later that I realized I could say no to his plans and begin to reach for my own dreams.

I've heard stories from friends and colleagues who struggled with parent-child relationships, but those were not my stories. My parents always loved and nurtured me, even when I upset or confused them. And some of my behaviors as a child were both puzzling and worrisome. Over the years, my mother would often gaze at me and ask, "Where did you come from?" I often wondered that myself.

In retrospect, I believe that many of my so-called peculiarities and worrisome behaviors were related to my having been adopted. I think that, at some primitive level, I always knew I was different, an outsider, and therefore vulnerable to the whims of others. Although my parents never for a moment gave me any reason to believe that they would ever reject or abandon me, I believed that, having been abandoned once, it could happen again. I knew what my birth mother had done, and for a long time I pretended to understand why. There were few acceptable choices for unwed mothers in 1952. But understanding that this had more than likely been her circumstance didn't alleviate the pain and confusion I felt about her choice.

While writing this book, I spoke to other adoptees and I read many articles on adoption. What I learned was that feeling different was something many adoptees had in common. Those differences often started with the obvious fact that you are the only one who doesn't look like anyone else in the family. John, one of the adoptees I spoke to, said, "I never looked like my parents and other people would say 'you clearly don't resemble those people.'" Cheryl, another adoptee, commented that her son was the first person she'd ever looked like. "I have a picture of him at two years old," she said, "and people think it is me. So that's very cool, and you know, it is such a funny thing that most people don't think about." But physical differences are just the tip of the iceberg. Deeper questions about how and where one fits in are often just below the surface. One gentleman, whom I'll call James, said that he had been assigned a school project about family heritage, and when he asked his mum about their family heritage she said, "Your Dad is Irish and my family is from Canada." He then asked her about his birth family, and she said, "Your mother was Hispanic, your father was German. Just tell them you are American."

"She was glossing over it," he sighed, "and that was when I began to realize that, yeah, I was different."

In an article called *Adoption: Trauma that Lasts a Lifetime* [1]Vicki Rummig wrote, "Physical differences are not the only ones that are noticed. A difference in

---

[1] www.vsn.org/trauma.html

personality or talents may further misplace the adoptee from her family." She then goes on to say, "I have described this feeling as feeling like my adoptive family is in a big circle but I am on the outside looking in." That made perfect sense to me. I looked different from my brothers—Verd had blond hair and blue eyes, Dan was tall with light grey eyes and I was small with dark hair and dark eyes. The physical differences were the first ring in the circle but the deeper, invisible circles are even more powerful. And I always felt different, out of step somehow.

One of the behaviors that worried my parents was crying in my sleep. When I was very little, probably three years old, I remember my dad waking me up from one of my crying jags to ask me what was wrong. I didn't have an answer for him that night or any other night, and that was frustrating for him. How could I not know why I was crying? I remember the exasperation in his voice and I really wanted to be able to answer his question, but I couldn't put the feelings into words. I didn't know why I was sad; I just was. Lesli Johnson, a marriage and family therapist who works with adoptees, adoptive parents, and birth parents, said in her article, *Ten Things Adoptees Want You to Know* that, "When we are young, we don't have the ability to identify our experience and articulate our feelings," and goes on to say that, "When an infant or child is separated from his or her birthmother, it is undeniably traumatic. All at once familiar sights, sounds and sensations are gone, and the infant is placed in a dangerous situation—

dangerous, that is, as perceived by the infant."[2] There was no obvious reason for my night tears or my sadness. So perhaps Johnson is right; maybe somewhere deep inside I was missing the movement and the sound of my birthmother that I experienced in the womb.

I also talked to myself, and when I was eight years old, I had an imaginary playmate, a blue horse named, naturally enough, Blue. Many children have imaginary playmates but I was the first one in our family. And I think my parents were really concerned about how real this creature seemed to be to me and how it was invading the 'real' world. Blue liked to sit in my father's chair and I could be heard to shout, "No, don't sit there. Blue is there." as my Dad was about to settle into the chair. My parents would try to convince me that the horse was just imaginary so it was okay for Dad to sit in his own chair, but I was having no part of that. Blue was real to me. He lived behind the freezer and popped out when my parents least expected him. He was also a lot of fun. He could dance, and there was nothing better than when Blue slipped out from behind the freezer so that we could dance together. My mum and dad had a great record collection, and after we kids went to bed, they would put on one of their favorites—maybe Cole Porter, Benny Goodman, or Nat King Cole—and dance. I pretended to be asleep, but when the music drifted up the stairs, I would slide out of bed and sneak down to the kitchen. The stairs were at the front of the house, across from the kitchen and the living room was at the back of the house-easy to slip

---

[2] https://www.huffingtonpost.com/lesli.johnson/
adoption_b_2161590.html

past without being seen. Blue would hear me coming and he would be waiting for me. He stood tall on his two back legs with his front hoofs gently on my shoulders, and we would dance. Quietly, carefully, and with pure joy, but never for long because we didn't want to get into trouble. Dancing with Blue was magic. His breath was soft; it smelled like honey.

It would be a few years before I was able to put my feelings of being an outsider, of not belonging to this family, into words. But for as long as Blue was behind the freezer, I knew I had someone to whom I belonged and with whom I was safe. Blue was around for about a year and when he disappeared, I missed him, but I think my parents breathed a sigh of relief. I don't know why he showed up in the first place and I don't know why he left me when he did, but I can still see him, smell him, and feel the shelter he gave me.

As a small child, I was constantly on the move, climbing cupboards and drawers to see what was in them or on them. My mother put bells on my shoes and named me "Miss Up-to." When the bells stopped ringing, she started to run. If the bells were tinkling, she knew I was wandering around, presumably playing but when all went quiet, there was a good chance I was up to something. She just wanted me to be a good child, one who didn't cry at night for no reason, get into mischief or make up imaginary creatures. She wanted what she thought of as a normal child.

One particularly perplexing situation occurred when I was eight and decided to make a magic wand. I had read about magic wands in a children's magazine and I wanted one for myself. I gathered the necessary components described in the magazine: a stick twelve inches long, string, three buttons, salt, and small bits of paper ripped up like confetti. My mother's eyebrows knitted together with concern watching this process, but she never interfered. Once I had everything I needed, I went outside to dig a hole. I had to put all the pieces in a deep hole in a specific order, cover them up, and leave them to rest for a year. At the end of the year, the wand would be ready to dig up. The trouble with my plan was two-fold. One, we lived on an airbase in northern Canada where the ground was frozen for eight months or nine months of the year, so digging a hole in February was very difficult. But, with a small spoon and tremendous determination, I did it. My mother watched through the kitchen window, not saying anything but not helping either. Even at eight years old, I recognized the worry on her face, but I kept digging anyway. The second problem with my plan occurred in June when my father was transferred again, and we moved to southern Ontario. At that point, my wand was not yet ready to be retrieved, so I had to leave it behind. I cried as the plane took off, and while my parents tried to reason with me, I was inconsolable. They were astounded by the power of my imagination, but I knew that the magic wand would have helped me answer my questions about whom I really belonged to. They told me later that they'd hoped I would forget about it in time, but I never did. Even now I wonder about the power of that magic wand buried deep in the Canadian north. Would it have helped me figure out who I was and to whom I belonged? I was counting on it!

Except for when I was dancing with Blue, the one place where I felt completely at peace was on the ice. I loved to skate. It was my favorite thing to do as a kid and I skated whenever I could. There is an old eight-millimeter movie of me going ice skating for the first time. I was five years old when Santa brought me skates, and my Dad took me to the rink on Christmas Day. It was an outdoor rink on the prairies—very cold, but I didn't care. I was wearing a crushed raspberry colored velvet coat and leggings with a matching hat. The coat and hat were trimmed with white bunny fur, and the hat was tied snugly under my chin. I looked like a fragile porcelain doll, but I wasn't made of porcelain and I wasn't a doll. I was alive and I was fearless. I stepped onto the ice and the rest of the world slipped away. It was breathtaking, exhilarating. My feet glided, one in front of the other, as if they had done this a thousand times. The rest of my body was simply along for the ride. I twirled, I hopped. I raised my face to the sun and spun, arms wide. I was never happier than when I was on the ice. I skated for years and that feeling of peace was always there. I was never an excellent figure skater but I skated hard. I wasn't destined for greatness, but the joy I felt simply being on the ice was what counted. The questions about where I came from or why I was left behind melted away. Every worry, every fear slipped away. In a weird way being just okay as a skater gave me the freedom to simply skate. Nothing to prove, no one to impress. I owed no one anything when I was skating. It was the place I felt the most at peace for much of my life. Even in later years the smell of the ice would carry with it a sense of peace, a peace that eluded me most of my days.

Another of my defining characteristics that I am convinced is related to my being an adoptee is the fact that

I have always been a keen observer of others. I was constantly surprising my parents with what I remembered about people and places. I could always tell them what color the walls were in Mrs. Maclean's bathroom, what color the carpets were in Mrs. Bennet's house, how many cupboards were in my grandmother's kitchen. I could draw the floor plan of every house I had ever visited. While all of this was pretty useless, if amusing information, I also watched people to see if I could figure out what they were feeling. I listened to what they said and tried to figure out if their words matched the story I saw on their faces. This watchfulness grew into a skill of sorts, and ever since I was a child friends have sought me out for guidance on a variety of topics. When I was a teenager, they would ask my advice about boyfriends, school troubles, parent challenges. Then, as now, I seemed to be able to provide helpful advice. But I believe that my powers of observation also served to protect me from the rejection I always felt might be lurking just around the corner. If I could figure out what others were thinking or feeling, I would be able to respond in a way that was pleasing to them so that they'd want to keep me around. It is not uncommon for adoptees to refer to themselves as 'people pleasers,' and I completely understand that.

In the end, however, no matter what I was up to, no matter how concerned my parents might have been about my oddities, they accepted me for who I was and seemed genuinely content to have me in their company. That was their special gift to me. And yet, in spite of their unconditional love, I wondered who my birth parents were and why they had left me behind. What could I have done that was so bad?

Chapter Two
Secret Stigma

How did I wind up in an orphanage anyway? My parents told me I was special, that I had been chosen. But even as a young child I was aware that sometimes, something chosen could also be returned. I remember being with my mother when she bought shoes and then returned them a few days later because she decided she didn't want them. In a moment of great clarity, I thought— *my mother chose those shoes and then changed her mind. Would my parents change their mind and give me back like my mother did with those shoes?* I was only about four years old, but the memory lingered for a long time. And, just because I was chosen didn't mean we talked about how or why I was eligible to be chosen. At the time of my birth, out-of-wedlock pregnancies were often kept secret. Women would go into hiding until their child was born. John, one of the men I spoke to said, "You can probably imagine, back in 1956ish you know there's a young girl who is pregnant and, my God, we've got to get her out of here. Let's send her off to Colorado, let her live in the wilderness and deliver this child." Paul, another adoptee, said that his mother was living in Winnipeg when she got pregnant and went to Toronto to have him. As I learned later, my own birth mother was living in Saskatoon but left when she found out she was pregnant, ending up in Vancouver to give birth. I began life as a mistake, and everything about my birth was shrouded in secrecy.

My brother Verd rarely spoke to me about my adoption, but once, when I was seven years old, he hurt me and, shocked by his own behavior, was frightened of what might happen if I told our parents. "You can't tell Mum and Dad what happened," he warned me. "It will destroy our family and it will be your fault if that happens." Even at that age I wondered if he meant that I would be the one to bear the blame because I was adopted and he wasn't; I could be sent away and he would get to stay. Just because you were chosen didn't guarantee that you got to stay. My birth mother gave me away and my adoptive parents could too. I wasn't going to take that chance, so I never said a word about what Verd did to me and I got to stay. There is no doubt that these were my perceptions but in that moment in time, those perceptions were my reality. When I spoke to James, he told me that his father had actually said, "You are adopted and we can take you back for a refund any time." He had hoped then that his dad had been joking, but, at the same time, he harbored a deep-seated fear that there was always a chance it might happen.

While my parents certainly never threatened to send me back, my dad's mum, who was a lovely lady and always kind to me, did warn me one day when I was nine years old that, "You better be good or they will send you back." Today I realize she didn't really mean it, and that it was an easy way to intimidate an adopted child who was misbehaving (although I have no recollection of what I might have done to warrant such a warning). But at the time I was certain it was true.

Because of the stigma attached to bearing a child out of wedlock—and the concomitant stigma attached to the 'bastard child'—adoptions were historically conducted in secret, and that secrecy did not necessarily benefit the child. In fact, although many families certainly loved and cared for their adoptive children, in the early years of adoption, families usually took in children to provide additional labor. It wasn't until 1851 that the state of Massachusetts (followed in Canada by New Brunswick and Nova Scotia in 1873 and 1896 respectively), passed the first formalized adoption laws based on protecting the welfare of the child rather than the interests of the adults who were involved in the transaction.

By the 1920s, legal adoption had become a widely recognized tool of the modern child welfare system. But it was still a largely secret business, with each set of parents agreeing to maintain the privacy of the other. In the decades that followed, social workers began to seal adoptions records. Birth parents (or, more commonly, the birth mother) could not know who had adopted their child, and the adoptive parents could not know the identity of the birth parents. It remained up to the adoptive parents to tell (or not tell) the child that he or she was adopted. The child sitting in the middle of this social contract had no say. Their future lay in the hands of adults who professed to 'know best.' The child's past was erased leaving in its wake an empty space where their new life could be scripted.

It wasn't until late in the twentieth century that Bastard Nation, followed by other adult adoptee support groups, began to advocate for changes in the laws that would open adoption records to adoptees seeking information about their birth parents. The first open records law was passed by Oregon State in 1998, but even today both the Canadian and American legal systems continue to make searching difficult. In some states, for example, adoptive parents are still required to sign a waiver allowing their adult child to search for his or her birth parents. For his book *The Adoption Triangle,* published in 1978, Arthur Sorosky spoke to adoptees about the effects of being unable to obtain information about their birth parents. One of his interviewees told him that, "As an adult, he could do anything freely without his parents' consent, but he had no right to ask questions or receive answers about his biological heritage unless they allowed it." (p.23)

Similarly, John (one of the adoptees I spoke to) said that he had "called Catholic Services but they never returned my call. Then I wrote them again. I got a letter back saying they were prohibited from talking about it so please don't contact us again. Some years passed and I called them again. This lady called me back and said we could meet but we have to meet in person. She was very candid, saying there was nothing she could tell me at that time but there was a process, so let's meet. What I realized was that I was the one being interviewed to see if I was a nut job." No one made it easy.

In the 1940s and 50s, however, the privacy laws were still firmly in place, and adoption was becoming an increasingly acceptable alternative for mothers who could not keep and care for an unwanted child. Homes for unwed mothers offered young women a place to stay while they waited for their baby to be born. If she was still a minor, her family might send her to a facility in another town for the duration of her pregnancy, after which she would return home and resume her life as if the birth had never taken place.

Very often these homes were attached to religious institutions such as the Catholic or United church. Salvation Army homes also did a brisk business. In addition to care for the expectant mother, some homes also provided care for the babies after birth. Or, alternatively, the babies went to an orphanage until they were, hopefully, adopted. Prospective adopting parents could go to the orphanage and look over the newest batch of babies to see if one looked good to them. Pretty baby girls and handsome baby boys were the first picked. Imperfect babies stayed longer, sometimes for years and, in some cases, their whole childhood. Carla, a woman I spoke to who had been adopted as a newborn said, "I thought of my parents walking into a grocery store and picking me out of all the children in the aisle."

While there were social workers involved in the adoption process, it was the individual religious community that had the final say regarding the placement of a child. On paper, the process appeared to be well managed, but there were still many mistakes in the records and ways to avoid the system altogether. Adoptions could still be done privately, with little or no formal documentation, in which case a baby might just disappear into another family, and that was the end of it. Daniel, one of the adoptees I spoke to was the product of a private adoption. Two doctors got together and decided that he should be taken from his mother immediately. She was a teenager and her parents believed that keeping the baby would ruin her life. She had no say. These two doctors did a deal behind closed doors, with minimal consultation and the child moved from room A to room B thus removing the 'problem' for the birth mother's family. No paper work required. And some organizations made the process horrific for the birth mother. The Salvation Army home in Toronto insisted that the women physically hand their babies to the adopting parents. Paul's mother was one of those young women who had to do this. She had to walk up to the adopting parents and place her son into their arms and then watch them drive away. He said, "I guess it was kind of like a therapeutic slash punitive prank." I think it was heartless and cruel.

Following the end of World War II, men returned home from the war, eager to normalize and move on with their lives after the brutality they had witnessed. Marriage numbers increased and the baby boom was born—along with a boom in adoptions. The economy was good and people wanted to have larger families. Meanwhile, unwed women were still getting pregnant. Abortion was illegal and keeping a child was rarely possible without family support. Formalized adoption was meant to make giving up illegitimate children easier for everyone. Families didn't have to take in these children anymore. With religious organizations and Social Services offering care for infants and the promise of a happy new future for them, women had what appeared to be, a new viable option. But the stigma attached to giving birth to a 'bastard' was still very much alive and even if a child was adopted, the label still applied. No matter how pretty, handsome, healthy, or smart you might be, as an adoptee you believed you were unwanted because the fact remained—your mother had given you away. Society's label stuck— you were a bastard, forever. Adoptive parents (or, at least, those who told their child that he or she was adopted) did their best to turn that negative into a positive by emphasizing the idea that he was 'special' or she was 'chosen.' Unfortunately, however, that narrative didn't necessarily work out as planned. Among those interviewed by Sorosky (1978), one male adoptee pointed out that he "felt that it worked both ways; that there were certain qualities about me that one set of parents chose, while the other must have rejected me for the same qualities."

I never bought into the idea of being chosen. I believe that I was just in the right place at the right time. In fact, my parents had been about to adopt twin boys the year before I was born, but the adoption fell through. They reapplied and got me. The Cambridge Dictionary defines luck as "good things that happen to you by chance and not as a result of your efforts or abilities." Lucky is an adjective that follows from that definition and so, to my mind I wasn't so much chosen as I was—well, a lucky girl.

The stigma of illegitimacy and the secrecy about my birth parents fueled my almost paralyzing need to be good. If I was good my parents would keep me. The sense of shame I always felt about being given away by my birth mother fed this need as well.

I never asked my parents if they had ever considered sending me back, and I never asked what being good meant to them. I simply adjusted my behavior to ensure that I was being good. I learned what being good meant by reading my prayer book, which described good children; I listened to our priest talk about good children; I listened to my parents' descriptions of the actions of other people's good children and tried to act like them. Being good became central to the core of my character.

In their article *Lifelong issues in Adoption*, Deborah Silverstein and Sharon Kaplan stated, "Adoptees seldom are able to view their placement into adoption by birth parents as anything other than total rejection. Society promulgates the idea that the 'good' adoptee is the one who is not curious. At the other extreme of the continuum is the 'bad' adoptee who is constantly questioning, thereby creating feelings of rejection in the adoptive parents." I was fixated on being 'good,' accepting whatever came my way, especially bad things—as if it were my due. Somewhere in my very early years a picture lodged in my mind of a bad baby—a baby who did something so wicked their mother gave them away. I didn't know what I could have done but luckily, I got a second chance. I had new parents and if I wanted them to keep me, I better be a 'good' child. That meant not asking too many questions about my adoption because it seemed to upset them. And I didn't want to upset them—ever. And, I never wanted my adoptive parents to think I was rejecting them. Heaven forbid! What a muddle.

In her *Huffington Post* article, Lesli Johnson's article *Ten Things Adoptees Want You to Know* (Huffington Post, January 11, 2013) she says, "Often, adoptees acclimate in one of two ways. Some might test the limits, trying to discover if they are going to be abandoned again. Others acquiesce to situations—hoping if they go along, they will keep their place in the adoptive family." And Vicki [3]Rummig refers to the compliant 'perfect' child as one who is trying to live up to his or her 'chosen' status. While I worked hard to be the perfect child, the good child, James walked the challenger's path—pushing boundaries, testing rules, questioning everything. "I was not the all-American boy," he told me. "If there was a dumb decision, I made it." He was the rebel child, testing his parents' commitment to him every step of the way. He never really believed he was good enough for them. In-spite of their love, he was constantly waiting for the day when they would give in, give up and say, "You were right all along. We never loved you." Either way—being the good child or the bad child—the behavior reflects a need for reassurance. Will you keep me no matter how I act or will you give up on me like 'she' did? A bleak way to live your life.

For me, one requirement for being good was not discussing the subject of adoption outside our immediate family. When I was about ten years old, I told a friend that my brother Dan was adopted. When he found out, he was about as upset as I'd ever seen him. I remember his face, red and blotchy, with tears in his eyes. It was one of the few times I ever saw him cry. My mother was furious with me, stating in no uncertain terms, "You will not speak about Dan's adoption to anyone ever again." Those words were burned into my brain, a reminder that our family affairs, specifically our adoptions, were not for public discussion.

---

[3] https://www.jigsawqueensland.com/ lifelong-issues-in-adoption

If that was the case, it seemed clear to me that adoption must somehow be shameful. If Mum had told Dan it was no big deal, perhaps I would have looked at it differently as well. But her reaction (not to mention Dan's) was so intense and so negative that it left me feeling dirty. With the benefit of hindsight and maturity, I wonder if her anger was tied up with her own feelings of unworthiness because she and my Dad couldn't have their own children. But no matter what prompted her words, they stuck. Being adopted was something to hide. In an online article entitled, *Why Children Need to Know Their Adoption Story,* Jayne Schooler writes, "When adopted children grow up in an environment where no one talks about the past or mentions their birth family, they receive the message. Do not ask." That was the clear and lasting message in our home. Do not ask. Do not tell.

From that day on, I rarely spoke about my adoption to anyone outside my family. In fact, I hardly ever spoke about it inside my family, not even with Dan. I wanted to talk to him about what he felt but I didn't dare ask.

My goal was to show my parents that they had made a good choice, that I was a good pick. But the path I chose was a difficult one for me. Always trying to be a good child prevented me from trying new things, asking difficult questions, or pushing back, because I believed that if I did any of those things, my behavior would be interpreted as ungrateful. Rather than take that risk, I stood still when I should have moved, stayed quiet when I should have spoken. I didn't ask questions because I feared the answers. I watched; I learned from others. But I didn't take risks, and I was never brave.

I thought that being an observer of life was something to be proud of. But I now realize that being a good observer often meant I was a poor participant. I didn't step into life as readily as many of my peers. Whenever I took an aptitude or personality test, I scored low as a risk taker but very high as an observer. When I was a graduate student, we had to complete a team participant assessment tool. We were presented with a series of questions that ranked what kind of team mate we would be. It focused on areas where you excelled and areas where you could improve to be part of a team. My score as an observer was so high that my professor asked if he could share it with the class. "This is an amazing score," he said. "She is watching you all the time. I mean, all the time." He then pointed out that people who are exclusively observers are not contributing their thoughts and ideas to the team, and that this would, ultimately, be detrimental to the team as a whole. It was like a lightning bolt had hit me—I was afraid to be a participant. Observing was safe; participating was risky. That was my approach to life.

As a teenager, my brother Verd was a risk taker. He pushed back when my father's rules bound him too tightly. I remember one weekend when he and a friend went on a road trip, driving from Toronto to Halifax and back, 2,232 miles, in 48 hours. There was nothing wrong with taking a road trip like that, except that he didn't tell anyone. When he returned, I hid behind my bedroom door and listened. I wondered what was going to happen to him. I knew my parents couldn't send him back to the orphanage because he wasn't adopted, but there were still fireworks. My father was angry and he was shouting. I hated shouting and still do. I decided right then that there would be no unexplained road trips for me.

I kept to the safe path for a long time. But, interestingly, I was also a sneaky kid. I hid things from my parents, told half-truths, and somehow believed that, as long as I didn't get caught, I was being good. I even tried shoplifting. I had a friend who was an expert! She stole everything she could and never got caught so I thought, why not? I picked up a lipstick and put it in my pocket. Then panic set in and I quickly put it back but not because it was wrong to steal. It was much simpler in my mind. If I was caught, I would have a black mark against my 'good' name. And I never, ever wanted that to happen because my parents would then have the perfect reason to give me back, proving that my birth mother had been right all along—I did deserve to be rejected by her because look, I was a bad seed. Convoluted thinking to be sure! I was a young adult before I took a hard look at those behaviors and recognized them for what they were: my own way of pushing back against perfection. The most important thing was to please my parents, and if that meant sneaking around or lying with a smile, so be it.

That way of thinking followed me into my marriage and, at least in the early years, guided my behavior as a wife. I didn't lie to Bob or hide things from him like I did when I was a little girl but I did stay silent when I should have spoken up. I could have pushed back, been braver but I wasn't. I was always afraid of disappointing him because that could lead to rejection. And if he rejected me, I would be out on the street, homeless and destitute—amazing where my imagination could carry me! As time passed, for reasons I didn't understand nor question, he became more insistent that I stand in his shadow when we were out in public, both figuratively and literally. I simply complied. This was important whether it was a work function or a social situation. He would warn me ahead of time to stay quiet, say as little as possible, smile politely. I dreaded any events, monitoring my behaviour at every turn. If I did speak up too much, engage with people too much, he would reprimand me on the way home and then, once the scolding was over, not speak to me again for three or four days.

One event in particular stands out. We were guests at an anniversary party for family friends. It was a lovely affair and because I knew a few of the guests, I was chatting away like a magpie. Bob was quiet during the meal and I thought it was simply because he didn't know as many people as I did. And because I was busy talking, I was unaware of his building anger. But as we walked back to the car at the end of the evening, he was silent. I knew that I had displeased him, I just wasn't sure how. Once inside the car, he told me that I had humiliated him in front of our hosts, that I had talked too much, spoken out of turn and I should have left the talking to him. He was furious. I was confused. I didn't believe I had embarrassed him, but in that moment, it didn't matter what I thought. His fury overshadowed everything. I had stepped out of his shadow. He didn't speak to me again for seven days—the longest silence yet. And I was distraught. I didn't know how to fix this mess and all the old worries about being rejected washed over me. After all, I was a good wife and good wives don't make mistakes. It didn't occur to me until much later that maybe it was his mistake—not mine.

As much as I never felt good enough for my husband, I prayed that I would be good enough as a parent. The need to be good took on a whole new meaning for me after my first child, Shawna, was born. For one thing, I was afraid that because I was adopted, I would be a bad mother. After all, my birth mother must have rejected me for a reason. Perhaps she intuited something about my character I didn't, something that would affect my ability to parent. And perhaps there was something in my heritage that would affect my daughter down the road. I worried that I might have some hidden genetic flaw that would be passed to her, or some weird behavior that would only manifest itself later in life. I worried about all kinds of things, and with no one to ask, the fear persisted. Would I be a good parent, or at least good enough?

Chapter Three
Living with the Fallout
from Shame

I believe that shame, a toxic cocktail of guilt, regret, and sadness, is a factor in the life of every adopted child even though it is not an issue often discussed during the "Hey, guess what, you are adopted" conversations adoptive parents have with their children. One blog, entitled *Adoptee Rage,* states that, "Each adopted child-adult adoptee can never escape being adopted. The worst thing that could happen to a child. The shame of everyone knowing your most humiliating personal secret is the worst thing in the world for adopted children. We are marked forever by being abandoned from our biological parents, heritage and culture." [4]

I know that I grew up believing that being adopted was something to be ashamed of. I thought I must have done something terribly wrong as a baby, and whatever I had done landed me in the adopted category. I didn't understand

---

[4] http://adopteerage.blogspot.com/2015/03/adoption-is-shame-that-last-lifetime.htm

what I'd done, but I knew one thing for sure: being adopted was a black mark on my record. No matter what words my parents used to describe me—special, chosen, picked—they also said or didn't say many other things that made me feel otherwise. They didn't want to talk about the circumstances of my adoption. They told me my birth parents were dead (which turned out not to be true, at least in so far as my mother was concerned; I never did find out who my birth father was or what had become of him), and they thought that would be all I needed or wanted to know. Any further questions I might have were always discouraged. Perhaps that's why my brother Dan reacted so strongly to my telling people he was adopted. When I think about the degree to which my own shame influenced my life, I wonder if he felt the same way and pushed the feelings down as far as possible, as I did. I was never brave enough to ask him.

Of course, friends of my parents and our extended family knew I was adopted. I knew that they knew, and by the time I was six or seven, their knowledge began to increase the depths of my shame. Chosen or not, no matter how special I was, the fact remained that my real mother had given me away. And since no one would tell me why, I made up my own reasons, none of them good. I was a scrawny baby, bald and sickly. Maybe that was a good enough reason to walk away. I was born a girl. Maybe that was the reason. I wasn't the smartest kid in my class, so maybe my birth mother somehow knew somehow that I wasn't going to be a star. The most persistent message I repeated to myself was that I simply was not worth keeping. And the fact that a lot of other people, including grandparents and family friends who had been around when

I was adopted, knew my story (probably better than I did) just added to my shame. It also didn't help that, at family gatherings, I'd hear an aunt or a cousin whisper, "she's the adopted one" when they thought I was out of earshot. Their words echoed in my head because I thought they were said with a sense of pity and a touch of censure. When I was a young newlywed, my mother-in-law rekindled those old feelings when she referred to one of her nephews as "...that's the one they adopted. He has always been trouble." And even though the words were not spoken I heard "what more could you expect from a bastard?" I didn't know the young man and he may very well have been trouble, but was that because he was adopted? She certainly thought so. It made me angry, defensive, and I wondered what she thought about me. I felt shamed when people spoke about adoptees like they were some lesser kind of beings, who for some reason were expected to be bad people, the rotten eggs in the family. But as always, I pushed my fury down, stayed silent—not brave enough to challenge my mother-in-law's assumptions or anyone else's for that matter.

When I was preparing for university, for example, my father told me I should study science. My brother Dan had studied sciences, and if it was good enough for Dan, it should be good enough for me. I wanted to be a kindergarten teacher, but I did what my father wanted. Instead of education, I studied theoretical mathematics, a scientific approach to math and in my mind, that was close enough to what Dan studied to count as being a 'good' daughter. And frankly, I didn't like it much! I did alright in class but I was no math whizz.

Fighting for what I wanted had never entered my mind. And it was the same in my marriage. I married when I was twenty, and I believed that doing what my husband wanted, as my mother had done, was the key to being a good wife. Good wives didn't push back. And more than anything, I wanted to be a good wife, a good mother—one that didn't embarrass my husband or my children.

In the last chapter I talked about my need to be good and to please. These behaviours were based on my feelings of shame and assumptions about my own worth (or lack thereof). I held onto those assumptions as if they were truths, and even now, if I'm not careful, I can easily slide back into that abyss. It is exhausting.

The more I learn about issues surrounding adoption, the more I realize that my feelings were far from unique.

A number of studies have found that, while adopted persons are similar to nonadopted persons in most ways, they often score lower on measures of self-esteem and self-confidence (Borders, Penny, & Portnoy, 2000; Sharma, McGue, & Benson, 1996). This result may reflect the fact that some adopted persons may view themselves as different, out-of-place, unwelcome, or rejected. Some of these feelings may result from the initial loss of birth parents and from growing up away from birth parents, siblings, and extended family members. They also may be caused by an ongoing feeling of being different from nonadopted people who know about their genetic background and birth family and who may be more secure about their own identity as a result. Additionally, some adopted persons report that secrecy surrounding their adoption contributes to low self-esteem. [5]

In an open adoption blog post dated November 28, 2014, a woman named Kat wrote about meeting a new group of people for the first time, and speaking about adoptee rights and adoption reform: "I'm an adult," she said, "who can speak openly and loudly on all types of issues within adoption, but I still felt shame to say those words ["I'm adopted."] – to have someone know my mom didn't keep me. I haven't had to tell anyone in such a long time, the feeling that accompanied those words surprised me."

"I certainly felt shame," she continued, "and maybe it is something I will carry with me each time I have to tell another new person that I'm adopted. I was definitely reminded of the power of shame and how it can affect us."

For adoptees, shame is built on two equally strong and destructive feelings: rejection and abandonment. My birth mother left me behind, the ultimate reject, and, as a result, I have walked through life waiting to be rejected and tossed aside. I accepted that fate as my due because the first person who met me and was supposed to love me, had abandoned me. For a long time, I didn't really understand why I believed that. It was simply the story I told myself, and it made me guarded and watchful all the time.

One of my coping strategies for combating feelings of rejection and abandonment was to leave first. If a situation became difficult, I would feel an overwhelming need to get

---

[5] https://www.childwelfare.gov/pubpdfs/f_adimpact.pdf

away from wherever I was and whomever I was with. I took the idea of fight or flight to a new level, but the focus was almost always on flight. I didn't fight for myself very often as a child or a young adult. The thought of fighting for what I believed frightened me, perhaps because I believed that if I tried to fight, I would lose. I felt cornered during disagreements. I couldn't get my thoughts organized quickly enough to respond to verbal challenges, and the inability to organize an argument equalled immediate loss and, in a funny way, I equated losing with rejection. I was sure that fighting back could be catastrophic. I never gave much thought to possibly winning. Fighting meant there was a winner (them) and loser(me)—and no matter what, I was afraid the other person would walk away. It wasn't worth the risk. I would simply flee instead of facing up to the situation. Not necessarily well thought out to be sure but that didn't stop me. Sometimes I would physically remove myself and sometimes, I would just go silent and passive. If I quit first, withdrew in some way, I didn't have to deal with being rejected. In her book, *Journey of the Adopted Self*, Betty Jean Lifton writes, "To flee or to merge—that is the dilemma that faces adoptees." The desire to flee then gets wrapped up with the fear of abandonment and in the next breath panic sets in. And fleeing is different from giving in, but with the same result. Whether you flee from the situation or you give in, you are not standing up for yourself because you are afraid of the outcome. My choice was to run. It was as if a chain was tied around me,—invisible loops that were strong, impossible to break. The urge to flee was linked to my sense of abandonment and that linked to rejection—rejection linked to shame and shame looped back to the fear of abandonment. All circling back to a need to flee. The links held fast for a long time.

I was well into adulthood before I developed enough self-awareness to begin changing my behavior. But it was difficult, and I still sometimes find myself struggling to stay in tough situations.

The first time I didn't run when I wanted to was when Shawna was born. I remember the terror I felt on the drive home from the hospital. I wanted to set her down gently and leave. I didn't believe I deserved to have this beautiful little person in my life, and the need to flee was so overwhelming that I felt helpless in its presence. But then the beautiful creature looked at me, and I stayed. Fleeing from her was not an option. In a moment of clarity, I realized that to run from her would be to reject her, and I never wanted her to feel the intense sadness that came with feeling abandoned.

When my son, Matthew was born two and a half years later, the very same feeling came over me. But as I rocked him, his eyes held mine. We stared at each other for a bit. Then his eyes closed, my eyes closed, and the desire to run slipped away.

My children were the two people who helped me begin to break that pattern of flight. Over the years, there were times when I was overcome with a profound urge to flee from them, but I didn't. I might go for an hour, but I always came back. I grew to understand that the moments when I wanted to flee were the times I thought I was letting them down because I was a bad mother. Odd, often inconsequential things would trigger those feelings: saying no to a particular pair of shoes, to a sleepover date, or to guitar lessons. There were lots of those moments, especially during their teen years when, even though I knew I was making the right decision, I wanted to run. I knew that being a good mother meant making tough decisions but I still worried that my kids would reject me because they didn't like my rules, because their idea of a good mother was different from mine. And once those thoughts popped into my head I would be swallowed up by doubts and fears. During those years, I was scared in the deepest parts of my soul but had very little insight into why.

My fear of rejection was a key driver in my first marriage. In the early years, I didn't stand up to my husband when I should have, and, consequently, we developed unhealthy patterns. He would yell and I would withdraw, sometimes physically or sometimes, just emotionally. As the years passed, however, I began to push back. The shift began slowly when the children were born, but once I started to challenge him, it was too late. He was used to my going along with whatever he wanted, and he simply couldn't accept the person I was becoming. I tried to fix things between us, and at times he tried too, but we continued to grow apart until I woke up one day after twenty-four years of marriage and knew that I had to leave. I realized that I no longer had any reason to fear his rejection, since he had, in fact, already rejected the person I had become—and I was surviving. It was a revelation to me, and understanding that I would continue to be okay without him gave me the strength to move out.

In addition to my fear of rejection, another legacy I received with my adoption was a pervasive sense of guilt. Of course, when you're trying to be good all the time and never take any risks, there isn't much to feel guilty about.

But there was one big thing: I always felt guilty about asking my mother and father questions about my being adopted. Although I didn't know why, I knew that my questions made them uncomfortable, particularly my mother. She would watch me stumble awkwardly over my words, tears would appear in the corners of her eyes, and she would repeat what had become her stock response: "We don't really know anything. They told us your parents were dead." That response would generally shut me down, and I would wander away wondering who 'they' were and how they knew my birth parents were dead. And, even if my birth parents were dead, why couldn't I know who they were? Lots of questions rolled around in my head over the years, and other adoptees seem to have had similar experiences. One woman adoptee quoted in Betty Jean Lifton's book said, "I had been told my parents were dead…why had I not asked any questions about them? After all, dead people have names; they have relatives they have left behind; they have graves. Why had I behaved as if death had wiped out all traces of their existence?" [6]

As a child, I felt disloyal to my adoptive parents when I asked too many questions. They had, after all, chosen me, and I should be grateful. In truth, I was grateful; I just wanted more of my birth story than they knew or were willing to share. And even as an adult, asking about my adoption was still difficult. Others I spoke to had similar feelings of guilt about asking. James said, "I only asked a couple of times [about my adoption] and part of that was because when I did ask there was a sense of distress with

---

[6] Journey of the Adopted Self, p.5

Mom—that I even asked was emotionally distressing." Carla also said she felt guilty asking about her birth parents and commented, "I am so lucky to have the father I had. In my heart I thought it would hurt him."

But for me the need to know more about my birth parents and the circumstances surrounding my birth was more powerful than the any feelings of guilt. In fact, four of the adoptees I spoke to—John, Paul, Carla, and James—all said that they wouldn't search for their birth parents while their adoptive parents were alive. James might have been speaking for all of them when he said, "I wasn't going to search while my folks were still alive because I didn't want to hurt their feelings." I didn't want to hurt my parents either, but I searched anyway. I wasn't like my brothers. I looked different, I behaved differently, and I didn't feel like I fit in. I thought if I could just find out about my birth parents, I would understand more about myself. So, I kept asking questions that upset my mother and left me feeling guilty and ungrateful.

The strength of my mother's antipathy to any discussion of my adoption persisted throughout her life. I remember visiting her in the retirement home where she was living when she was ninety-six and I was sixty-four. She met me at her door, visibly upset, closed the door to her suite and said: "I have something to tell you and I don't know how you are going to take it. Last night at dinner Joyce [her table mate] said you were adopted. I never told her. I was very upset. Where would she hear that?"

"Are you sure she didn't say doctor?" I asked. "She thinks I'm a doctor."

"No," my mother said. "She said adopted. You know you are my daughter. Why would she say that? How does she know?" By that point in the conversation, I could feel myself sinking back into my old feelings of shame, rejection, abandonment, and guilt while my mother continued to mutter about Joyce.

"Mum," I said, "it's okay. It's the truth. I don't know where she heard it or why she brought it up, but it's okay."

"But you are my daughter," Mum cried, gripping my hand so hard it hurt.

I couldn't understand why she was so upset, but the good daughter needed to say something to cheer her up and change the conversation. "Yes, I am your daughter and I am adopted," I said. "Think of it this way—by the time you see Joyce tonight, she will have forgotten what she said. Everyone will have forgotten what she said." She looked at me and smiled. "That's true." And we moved on to other topics.

At that point, it was too late for me to ask why she didn't want to talk about my adoption. At ninety-six her mind was beginning to go, but she was clear that day about the fact that my adoption was a secret she wasn't going to discuss with her tablemates. I wondered whether she believed that being adopted wasn't wrong but talking about it was.

As I watched her prepare to go to dinner, I felt the old sensation of the chain-link circle return. Abandonment, rejection and shame squeezed my gut and I wanted to run. If it was so hard for her to admit to her friend that I was adopted, what pain had my own questions caused her over the years? The clang of the metal links reverberated inside my head, whispering a familiar refrain—you are not worthy. I leaned into her, kissed her gently on the forehead and left. A trail of jumbled and discordant feelings drifted along behind me as I left the building.

Chapter Four
The Search Begins

The last time I asked my parents about my adoption was in 1984, two years after that day at Mums and Tots. I had begun to search for my birth parents but hadn't made much progress, so I wrote my mother and father a letter, telling them what I was going to do. Since I hadn't yet learned anything useful, I didn't think it was necessary to mention that I had already begun. The trigger for this new attempt was a serious health crisis. I'd been having intense abdominal pain, and in order to find the illusive source of this pain, my doctors performed a new procedure that did, in fact provide the answer. My gall bladder was disintegrating from the inside out, which was highly unusual and the reason they'd had such a hard time arriving at a diagnosis. My body, however, reacted so badly to the procedure itself that I ended up with pancreatitis, a life-threatening illness. The only upside to all this was that I had a perfect excuse to ask more questions about my adoption. I'd been close to death, and I had no family medical history. How could my parents deny me?

Presenting my request in the context of my need for medical information provided a safe place from which to ask difficult questions, so I crafted my letter asking leading questions that all hinged on my wish to know more about my medical history. I took the chance of risking their unhappiness, but I wasn't brave enough to be totally honest about my request. I was constantly balancing my need for information against the pain my questions seemed to cause, and this time was no exception. It took a while to get the phrasing correct. I said that any information about my birth parents could help me and perhaps, help my children in case they ever experienced medical problems. I did lots of re-writes so that I wouldn't sound too needy, just needy enough. Finally, I signed off, mailed the letter and waited.

At the time, I was living in Vancouver, BC, and my parents lived in Kingston, Ontario, 2711 miles away. We wrote letters all the time and spoke on the phone only occasionally, perhaps once a month. Phone calls were expensive in those days, so we never called before six pm, when the rates went down. And whether I called them or they called me, my mother always took the lion's share of call time. My dad was lucky if he even got to say hello. He shouted in the background but rarely got to hold the phone for more than a minute. It never changed, except for six days after I mailed that letter. My phone rang at two o'clock on a Tuesday afternoon. There was no caller ID in those days, but I assumed it was a friend. I wasn't thinking about the letter I'd sent my parents and I certainly wasn't expecting to hear my father's voice. It felt like my heart stopped. Had something happened to my mother? Was she okay? Was he okay? "We're both fine," he said. He told me that they had received my letter. I held my breath. As he started to talk, what I braced to hear was, "You are an ungrateful brat. After all we've done for you, this is how you treat us? Why are you turning on us? We loved you, cared for you, and now you want to find them? Thankless child." What he actually said was, "We understand that this is important to you and we'll help you in any way we can. You know that Hugh (a family friend and my parent's attorney) was the lawyer who acted for us, so call him. Maybe he can help too." His voice was soft, kindness and concern appropriately dispensed. I thanked him profusely, over and over, all the while feeling needy and guilty. But my mother's voice was missing from this conversation. Silent.

"Is Mum okay with this?" I asked.

"Absolutely," he said.

"Can I talk to her?"

"No, not right now. We'll write you and give you any information we have." He paused for a moment and then added a cautionary note that lived at the back of my mind forever: "You may not find what you want; you may not get everything you wish for." Then he said, "Talk to you soon." And he hung up. Tuesday afternoon, expensive calling time and no Mum. A wave of guilt crashed into me, over me. Tears slid silently down my face. What have I done? What must she think? Guilt. The next letter that came was from Dad. He didn't have any new information to share with me. And my mother remained silent. She never talked about that letter, the phone call, or my request for information. The guilt about asking questions flipped over and over in my stomach. I hadn't fooled them. They knew why I was asking questions about my birth parents. The request for medical information was a ruse. And they still did their best to help. But the sadness those questions seemed to cause them was hard for me to bear. And because they were both so reluctant to talk to me about my adoption, I could only guess what they were really feeling. I wasn't brave enough to ask them why it was all so hard. But now that they knew what I was doing, I felt it would be okay for me to push forward.

My first step was to send a letter to the government of British Columbia requesting any information they had pertaining to my birth, including most importantly my birth parents' names, because the birth certificate I had listed my adoptive parent's names only. I wasn't sure what I would get back, because at the time I was adopted the Canadian and provincial governments both promised anonymity to any woman who gave a child into their care and were fierce in their resolve to maintain the secrets surrounding the birth and adoption.

When I finally received a response in the mail several weeks later, I sat on the steps of my house and stared at the envelope. I didn't feel ready to open it, and yet I couldn't *not* open it. This kind of approach/avoidance was an odd feeling, uncomfortable at best, frightening at worst, and one with which I would become more and more familiar as my search continued. Finally, I opened it. There was a cover letter explaining that the information being provided was considered 'non-identifying,' meaning that my birth parents would not be identified by name, but other information about them and their families was included. It also indicated that this was the information that had been provided by my birth mother when she decided to give me up for adoption. The next page was headed:

Background of Susan Kim Gunning

Your Mother:

Your mother was born in 1923 in Manitoba of Irish racial origin, and the Roman Catholic faith. After senior matriculation, she attended normal school, followed by three years of university. She enjoyed her employment as a teacher. Her main interests were writing, radio and dramatic work, including child drama and drama instruction.

The social worker described your mother as a very attractive looking girl, extremely well-groomed, intelligent and well educated. She had light brown hair, brown eyes and an olive complexion.

She was reticent in speaking about her family but she did tell the social worker that she was raised in Saskatchewan and had one brother, aged 19, who was in his second year [of] university and one sister, aged 17, in training as a nurse. It was also learned that her parents had separated, with her mother living in Saskatchewan and her father, somewhere in eastern Canada. No further details were provided.

Your Father:

The information we have about your father was obtained from your mother. He was 40 years old at the time of your birth and of Irish racial origin. He had a doctorate and was a university professor. He was six feet tall, with a heavy build, brown hair and eyes and had a very outgoing personality. His health and that of his family was said to be good. His main interests were sports.

Your father was married but had been separated for several years and was willing to get a divorce in order to marry your mother. However, because of your mother's firm religious beliefs, she did not wish to consider this proposal.

Your mother found it very difficult deciding upon adoption but, not wanting to marry your father and feeling unable to give you sufficient and proper care by herself, finally decided that adoption was the best plan.

You were born at St. Paul's hospital in Vancouver and weighed six pounds, 15 ounces at birth. It was a full-term pregnancy and the delivery was normal. Your mother came to British Columbia and Vancouver for her confinement and it was understood that she planned to leave the province after your adoption placement.

You were placed in your adoption home in December 1952. In the social worker's final report in January 1954, it was stated that you were progressing very well, were walking, and seemed very bright, taking a great interest in everything around you.

Your adoption was completed on February 19, 1954.

Receiving that letter from the government was one of the most emotionally charged moments of my entire search. As I read the words, tears slid down my cheeks, unbidden and unstoppable (there were a lot of tears throughout my search!). Breathing was hard. I swallowed and gulped, swallowed and gulped. I was so sad, so hurt, so lost all at the same time. I felt myself slipping away from the warmth of my kitchen and into the dark place in my mind where I went when I was lost.

As a child, even though my parents had told me I was adopted, I would sometimes pretend that I was my mother's real daughter and the story of my adoption was just that, a story. But now, for the first time, I had tangible, official confirmation of what I'd been told. Once again words like reject, cast-off, throwaway bounced around in my brain. I was reading one thing but my brain was telling me something else. Old stories kept reverberating, unbidden and yet, persistent. It felt as if I were being pummelled with pebbles. I sat still and let it happen.

After a few weeks of feeling sorry for myself (a place I drifted into way too often), it was time to keep moving with my search. I had heard a member of a group called the Canadian Adoptees Reform Association interviewed on the radio and I wondered if they would be able to help me. I contacted them and they invited me to attend their monthly meeting. I learned that the Canadian Adoptees Reform Association's mandate was to advocate for opening adoption records, making it easier for birth parents and children to reunite. I attended a couple of meetings before I worked up the courage to ask if they could help me with my search. They looked over the non-identifying information and suggested that I make a public appeal for information about myself. Perhaps someone in Vancouver would recognize me and come forward. I had no idea how to go about making a public appeal but they had ideas! They said I had an interesting story and a "good face." A good face? They said I would "look good on TV." *Whatever worked,* I thought. I was a novice in all this and I trusted that these people knew what they were doing. As a result, I appeared on two television shows. The first was a local evening news program for which my adoption was a 'human interest' story. A crew came to my home and filmed an interview with the host, who asked me a series of questions about my search for my birth mother: Why did I want to search? What had I learned so far? What did my adoptive parents think about what I was doing? The questions felt invasive and I had to fight the urge to run from the room every moment. Every nerve in my body was on high alert waiting for the host to ask what it really felt like to be a bastard child. No one ever asked me that but I never stopped expecting it. It was a weird experience, but I persevered because I was determined to do whatever it took to find my birth parents. The second interview was a provincewide live on-air interview that focused not only on my specific search but also on the whole question of whether or not adoptees and/or birth parents should be given access to sealed records. The host was a Scotsman known for his gruff and somewhat acerbic approach to interviewing. He was no different with me. He started the interview saying he believed that adoption records should remain sealed, that I didn't have the right to disrupt the status quo. He said that once a woman made the decision to give up a baby for adoption no one, including the child, had the right to intrude on her privacy. He was aggressive from the start and he asked difficult questions, but I pushed back. I talked about what it was like to be adopted and have no right to know where I came from. I said that as a baby, I had no part in a decision that changed the course of my life, but, as an adult, I should at least be able to find out who my parents were and understand the circumstances that made adoption the only path forward for them. I also talked about the loss of family history. I asked the host if he knew what part of Scotland his grandparents came from, and he acknowledged that, yes, he had information about both sides of his family reaching back for generations. I told him I had a blank wall behind me, a family tree littered with nothingness. My argument seemed to make a positive impression on him, and at the end of the interview he encouraged me to continue my search.

At the end of both shows I made an appeal for any information that would help me with my search, but I didn't receive a single helpful response. People called into the stations after each show encouraging me to keep looking, but no one had any specific tips about who my parents might be or how I might narrow my search. It was frustrating but not surprising. I appreciated the work of the Canadian Adoptees organization but decided it was time for me to refocus. From that point on my search became a solitary endeavor.

Since I now knew that my birth mother was Catholic and I was born in St. Paul's, a Catholic hospital, I assumed that I must have been baptized. According to the Catholic Church, babies go to heaven only if they are baptized, and I didn't think the Church would take the chance of losing even one soul. There were two Catholic churches near St. Paul's hospital, so I called the office of the archdiocese to see if either of them baptized the babies born at St. Paul's. As it turned out, both churches did baptisms for St. Paul's.

Phoning gave me a little information but I needed to go to the church and talk to the secretary at the archdiocese's office. When I arrived, I told her that I was adopted and I was looking for any information about my birth parents. I could tell that she was a bit shocked by my audacity, and she hesitated for a moment before telling me that all Catholic babies born in Vancouver who were going to be adopted were sent to St. Mary's hospital where the Sisters of Providence ran an orphanage. One of the adopting parents had to be Catholic, and they had to agree to bring the baby up in the Catholic faith. The adopting parents provided the names of prospective godparents and the child's new name, and the sisters then filled out a new baptismal certificate and forwarded it to the archdiocese office, where the new name was duly recorded. The original baptismal certificate then became part of the sealed file. She was clear about the fact that the records were sealed and there was nothing there for me to see. But I was equally clear: I wanted to see the baptismal records for 1952. She reluctantly agreed to let me see the available records and told me they were stored in the basement of the building. So down I went. I found a record book marked '1951–1952' and I began to slowly work my way through it. The information was amazing. The book listed the names and dates of all babies baptized. For those who were adopted, the records listed birth dates and birth names, and, even though the baptisms occurred before adoption took place, their adoptive names were also included.

Since the baptismal certificate my parents had listed only my adoptive name, Susan Kim Smyth, I was thrilled to see that the archdiocese's records also included birth names. But my excitement was short-lived. The records I was looking at stopped at the end January 1952, and I was born in September 1952. I went back upstairs to the church office with the record book in hand. "Where are the rest of the records?" I asked. The woman in the office looked up and said, "Those are all we have."

"But where is the rest of 1952?"

She just shrugged and repeated, "That is what we have." How could that be? I put the record book on her desk, turned, walked out of the office, down the long corridor to the church sanctuary, and sat down in one of the pews. The acrid smell of burnt candle wax from morning mass mingled with the fading aroma of incense. The combination turned my stomach and I knew I was going to be sick. I ran from the sacristy and threw up on the steps of the church, then sat for a few minutes waiting for the nausea to pass. Not a pretty sight but I was frozen, unable to move away from my own mess. Finally, I went back to the office to see if I could gather any more information about the missing records. Surely, they would have to be somewhere. The secretary wasn't too pleased to see me again, but she sighed and asked, "Which hospital?"

"St. Paul's," I answered.

"Oh," she said. "We didn't keep their records after January 1952."

"What? That doesn't make any sense. A priest lives at the hospital. Baptisms must be part of his job."

She said, "I'm not sure which church took care of the babies in 1952, but they probably kept the baptismal records." The secretary must have seen how upset I was because her expression changed and she said more kindly, "Try the hospital. Talk to Father John. He's the chaplain." St. Paul's was only a few blocks away. I had come this far. Would walking those few blocks make a difference? It was certainly worth a try.

When I asked Father John which church baptized their babies in 1952, he wanted to know why I needed the information. Sealed records were the backbone of the adoption process, and I didn't think he'd give me the information I needed if I told him the truth. So I lied. I looked him straight in the eye and said: "I was born here and I was a frail baby. The doctor was afraid I was going to die, so the priest was called in to baptize me. Now I've lost my original baptismal certificate and I want to get a new copy." He looked at me for a minute and then said, "St. Anthony's. It is on 70th." Miles away! "St. Anthony's? Why so far away when the cathedral is right over there?" He just shrugged his shoulders. I thanked him and left. I'd gotten the information I came for. I didn't need anything else from him.

When I got home, I phoned St. Anthony's and told the church secretary I needed a copy of my baptismal certificate. She asked me why. *Why?* "Because it belongs to me," I screamed. Except the scream was silent. I took a moment and said, "I'm getting married and I need it." Another lie. She asked me to write her a letter requesting the document. She gave me her name and the full address for the church. I wrote the letter using the name I'd been given when I was adopted. It was all I had. It had been more than thirty years, but my hope was that this church, like the archdiocese, maintained records that included both birth and adoptive names.

A week after I sent my request, an envelope from St. Anthony's arrived in the mail. In it was a handwritten copy of my original baptismal certificate with my birth mother's name and my original birth name. On the back of that slip of paper was a note that said: "Adopted by Phyllis and Reginald Smyth." Just like the archdioceses, St. Anthony's had set up a dual recording process. They had the original baptism information with the birth mother's name and an addendum with the adopting parents name. Given how secret the whole adoption process was supposed to be, receiving that paper was something of a miracle, but in the moment, I didn't think about why the secretary would have sent such 'classified information.'

I just held the piece paper in my hand and stared at it. My birth mother's name was Patricia Ann Murphy. My name was Mari Kim Murphy. Whether she knew it or not, the church secretary had provided a critical missing piece of my puzzle. I will be forever grateful to her.

It was time for the 'next' next steps. I had my mother's name and my name. Standing still—well, that wasn't an option, at least not for long. The idea of going backward didn't make any sense. How do you unknow what you know, undo your thoughts and feelings, pretend they didn't exist? I had only one choice—move forward. The familiar jumble of shame, rejection and abandonment nipped at my heart but something else was happening at the same time. I didn't know what it was and even today, it is hard to describe. Maybe it was because I had found my name and my mother's name—I am not sure. But I was excited to move forward, a sense of urgency rumbled in my gut. I had a new sense of purpose. I felt that there might just be a chance to find my birth mother after all.

The next phase of my search began with a trip to the Vancouver library, which had directories for every city in Canada that included the names of every person living at a specific address, including all members of a household. The non-identifying information I'd received from the government said my birth mother was from Saskatchewan and it said she went to Normal School which was what Teacher's Colleges were referred to that time. The only Teacher's College was in Saskatoon so I thought—maybe she lived in Saskatoon! I searched the Saskatoon city directories for 1950, 1951, and 1952. In 1950 Patricia Murphy lived with Disa Murphy, Catherine Murphy, and Ronald Murphy. The city directory also listed occupations for each person. Patricia Murphy was listed as a teacher. Ronald and Catherine were listed as students. Disa worked for the Canadian National Railway. I figured that Disa was Patricia's mother and that Catherine and Ronald were her siblings. The information was the same in 1951. Patricia, Disa, Catherine, and Ronald still lived at the same address. But in 1952 Patricia was not listed at any address in the Saskatoon directory.

The path to Patricia seemed to end in 1952, when she simply vanished. So, I changed focus and followed Disa. According to the Saskatoon directories Disa lived in Saskatoon until 1963. Then she too disappeared. I contacted the Canadian National Railway's employment office in Winnipeg and asked if they had an address for a Disa Murphy. I said she would be retired. She had worked with my father, and he wanted to contact her. I thought that would sound like a plausible reason for my request. The employment office redirected me to the retired employee office in Montreal. I wrote a letter to the Montreal office using the same story I had used with the employment office. It was a few months before they responded, but when they did, another pivotal piece of the puzzle fell into place. They said that after she retired, Disa moved to Red Deer, Alberta, to live with her daughter, Catherine Flanagan. I had found my grandmother and my aunt. This soaring moment of joy was followed by a crash of disappointment. Disa had been living in Red Deer, Alberta when she died on May 26,1983. As I read those words I sank slowly into a chair. I had hit yet another wall. For whatever reason, I thought that if Disa were alive, she would want to know about me and it would be okay to reach out to her. I could always spin a story for myself! And Catherine, well, in that moment I didn't think about contacting her. I had another story running in my head that contacting anyone but Patricia or her mother would be wrong. It was as if I would be breaking some kind of pact I had with her. Crazy, nonsensical, pure fabrication.

Some days I wondered why I was spending so much time on this; what was the point? And other days, it seemed that the search was a lifeline. My logical brain was constantly colliding with my emotional heart. But in the end, I carried on. I read the letter from the railroad again. If Disa died in Red Deer, perhaps there had been an obituary in the local paper. I knew I would find Catherine Flanagan in the Red Deer city directory, but in that moment she wasn't the one I wanted to find. I wanted to find Patricia Murphy. I hoped that the obituary would give me her name (I assumed she was probably married and had a different last name. I don't know why. It just seemed probable) and where she lived. I called my friend Anne, from the Mums and Tots group, and told her what I'd found out. Anne's sisters lived in Red Deer, and I thought they might be able to find out if there was an obituary for Disa. She called them, and they went to work for me. In two days, they had the answer I was looking for. The obituary said that Disa Murphy was survived by her daughter Patricia Campbell (nee Murphy), Calgary, Alberta, her son, Ronald Murphy, Toronto, Ontario, and her daughter Catherine Flanagan, Red Deer, Alberta.

There it was: Patricia Campbell (née Murphy), residence Calgary, Alberta. I could have been thrilled, but what I experienced in that moment were all the old familiar feelings of abandonment and shame flooding back. Here I was, sitting in my house holding a copy of my dead grandmother's obituary and wondering if she ever knew I existed. And there was Patricia, living a life without me. She had gone on with her life, leaving me behind. The reject. As the old feelings swirled around inside my head, I could feel myself sliding back into old stories of being unworthy, and even though part of me knew I was making up those stories, I couldn't break the spell. My guts were in turmoil and I began to experience overwhelming headaches. So, for the moment, I temporarily suspended my search. It had taken three years to get to this point.

The hiatus lasted a few months. Because I had shared my search with so few people, there wasn't anyone I wanted to talk with about the newest findings. A chill had settled in my bones, a numbness that lurked around the edges of my heart. I couldn't explain it or make it go away. My old story of 'poor me' was alive and well. Finally, something shifted in me, maybe I got tired of being sad. I wasn't normally a sad person and I didn't like the way it felt. And this inertia wasn't getting me to my goal. I felt ready to move forward again. But I didn't really know what to do next. I hadn't shared many of the details with anyone—not even my husband. Bob wasn't really aware of what I was doing, and that was as much my fault as his. He didn't ask many questions and I offered little information. To me, it was such a personal journey that it seemed easier for me to deal with my emotions privately and go it alone. Anne and Leah, my two friends from Mums and Tots, were the only people I talked to about the search, and even they didn't know all the details. But now that I had my birth mother's name and place of residence, I turned to Leah. She did some research and found an organization called Adoption Finders that helped to reunite adopted adults with their birth parents. Leah phoned them for me, told them my story, and they said they could help.

I met with a woman who explained their process to me. I think her name was Jean, but I am not even sure anymore. She said she would make the initial call, and if my birth mother was willing to have contact with me, Adoption Finders would help me with the next steps. If my birth mother refused the request for contact, they would end their involvement. I asked Jean to make the call, so she phoned, told Patricia who she was and why she was calling. Afterwards, Jean said that my mother—who had told her in no uncertain terms that she was always called Pat—at first went silent then asked her to call back in an hour. During the second call, it became apparent that Pat was in shock and also very angry. The government had promised to keep her secret a secret, and she had hidden my existence from everyone in her world. She'd planned, she'd schemed, she'd made up story after story for anyone who asked too many questions. She'd fabricated a whole new life, one with shadowy edges and moveable walls. For thirty-three years her secret had been safe. And then, in one phone call, the world she had so carefully constructed was fractured. Pat told Jean that she felt betrayed; she had been assured that no one, especially me, would ever be able to find her. She'd expected her decision to be respected. "This isn't right," she said. "They promised."

Chapter Five
Meeting Pat

Ultimately, that phone call turned out to be the beginning of yet another relationship complicated by guilt, secrecy, and shame. So many half-truths, outright lies, riddles—nothing easy or straight forward emerged.

After Pat recovered from her initial shock, she agreed to accept a letter from me. It was both wonderful and terrifying for me to be at the beginning of this new chapter in my life.

In my first letter, I assured her that I had no intention of disrupting her life by suddenly appearing at her door. I had a family, a life, and she needn't fear that I was on the hunt for a new one. Although I told her a little about myself, I was mostly focused on reducing her anxiety about having been found. When I look back, knowing what I know now, I can only imagine how terrified she must have been. And I grovelled. I would have, as they say, danced on the head of a pin if it meant she would write back.

In her return letter, she told me how relieved she was to know that I wasn't about to throw her entire life into chaos. She told me that her family didn't know about me. She wrote:

Your letter arrived last Wednesday and has been read and re-read numerous times. The original phone call was, to say the least, a shocker. The fragmented emotions are still in a state of mix-up. It never ceases to amaze me how resilient we human beings are—daily life carries on even though the inner workings are explosively chaotic.

My family is not aware of you and I must deal with this as I think best. Even as I pen these words, I am unsure of the actions I will take...."

After that, our exchanges settled into a kind of rhythm, a letter apiece every few months. We filled each other in on what was going on in our lives, but never attempting to dig much below the surface. I told her about my two kids—their personalities, what they loved to do. I tried to convey their quirks, and charms. I told her about my husband—what kind of work he did, a little about his family, and how we met. I described our life in a way that I hoped would continue to reassure her about my intentions. At that time, I was working as a preschool teacher. I told her I had graduated college with a degree in mathematics but my degree hadn't led to a job, so I went back to school and completed my studies in early childhood education. The information about Pat that I'd received from the government included the fact that she was a teacher, so I hoped that our shared vocation would provide the basis for a relationship between us. I explained that teaching allowed me to be there for my children when they came home after school, but also that I was becoming less satisfied with the work and wanted more of a challenge. As a result, I had begun volunteering a couple of evenings a week on the wards at BC Children's Hospital, playing with the kids or rocking babies so parents could take a break. I told her stories about some of my experiences at the hospital. In fact, I wrote about anything I thought might pique her interest in me. I sent pictures of me and my family. I was willing to try anything that might draw her in. And I was always balancing my desire to know more about her with the need to keep my letters light.

Pat was more forthright in her first letter than she was in any that followed. Her letters didn't give away very much. She skimmed the surface of topics but seldom slipped beneath the superficial. I wanted to dive below the everyday chatter that we usually shared, looking for deeper connections, hoping she wanted that too. I thought about asking her the tough questions that were on my mind—who was my father? Did anyone in her family know about me? How was her life affected by her choice? I knew it might be risky to ask these deeply personal questions so early in our relationship because I didn't know if she might disappear again, stop writing because I wanted too much from her. But I also wanted to be able to look back and know that I had at least tried to get answers. In the end, I didn't ask those questions. I wasn't brave enough. I was too afraid that asking for more than she was willing to give might just drive her away.

In addition, as much as I wanted those answers, I also feared them. I was afraid to get too close. What if my questions ended up destroying her life? Or what if there were secrets that would damage my life? When I spoke to other adoptees, they had similar fears. Carla said, "I think about my story and what it could be. You can be opening this can of worms that you wish you never did. I was so scared of that. And I wouldn't want to destroy somebody's life." Cheryl's comments were similar. She said, "It's a bit of a Pandora's box—you've got to go into it open to whatever happens and not just hoping for some particular outcome. I wasn't sure I was prepared to take on that kind of potential chaos." John completed his search but even he expressed that deep fear. He said, "You never know what you're going to get when you start down this kind of path and for the guy I actually consider to be my real brother, Brian, he never wanted to go down this path because he told me that he was afraid of the outcome." It seemed like we all had as many reasons to stand still as we did to move forward. And yet many of us did moved forward, taking that risk.

In hindsight, I see that I sometimes resisted intimacy with Pat as much as she did with me. What if she doesn't like what she reads? What if I say something that makes her glad she gave me away? What if—I had so many ideas about what Pat might do or not do, like or not like that it was simpler to retreat into surface chatter than it was to take a risk. I should have asked myself, what is the worst thing that can happen if you ask your questions? She would either answer them or not. And if she stopped writing, well, she stopped. She had walked away once before and I had survived. I would survive this too, however it turned out. But I didn't think about that at all. Instead, the old desire to flee was alert and ready to respond at a moment's notice. I didn't really trust this relationship any more than Pat seemed to.

I was, however, beginning to understand more clearly how being adopted had affected my life. On one hand, my adoptive parents were wonderful people and I wanted Pat to know I was okay. But, on the other hand, the years had taught me that the shame I felt because I was adopted, the pain that came from being rejected and abandoned, were also a part of who I was. I didn't wallow in the murkiness of shame all the time, but I believed that understanding Pat's side of the story would help me to understand myself better and, therefore, begin to let go of the shame. And I also thought that asking questions in a letter would make it easier for her to answer than if we were face to face. But, one way or the other, we still both managed to avoid the tough stuff.

She told me that she'd married and had three daughters, which didn't really surprise me. The only real shocker was that, three years after I was born, she named the first of those daughters Kim. She slipped that fact in between telling me she loved to garden and her husband's name was George. No doubt Freud would have a great explanation, but I just shook my head in disbelief. Robin and Miji (Marion Joan) were the next two girls but my focus was squarely on Kim. Pat named me Kim. Then she named her next daughter Kim. Why?

Over time, it became clear to me that if I were ever to get answers to my lingering questions, Pat and I would have to meet in person. I also understood that if such a meeting were to take place, I would have to be the one to make it happen.

In June of 1986, almost two years since I had written my first letter to her, I wrote Pat and told her I had an opportunity to come to Calgary in July. The Calgary

Stampede, a well-known annual rodeo event, was always held in July, and my friend Connie told me she was going to it. Going to the Stampede with Connie seemed like a plausible cover story to satisfy the curiosity of nosy neighbours who knew that I never went away by myself. I told Connie I would be visiting a friend in Calgary while she was there and perhaps we could get together. Having her in the same town at the same time felt like a safety net if things didn't go well with Pat. Since I really had no idea how it might go, I created a list of catastrophic possibilities. I never focused on what might go well. I maintained a very myopic focus on my relationship with Pat in the early years.

Waiting for Pat's reply gave me all the time I needed to panic about my request. What if she said no? What if she said yes? Which would be better? Worse? A letter arrived and, as I often did with letters from Pat, I simply stared at it for a while before I opened it. Over the time we had been writing, I always wondered if the newest letter might be the last, if that she would say she was going to stop writing, didn't want any further contact with me. This time was no different. But, as it turned out Pat said she would meet on the day I'd proposed, which triggered yet another wave of panic. She said to let her know where I was staying and she would meet me at my hotel room at noon on the Saturday. It was clear that she was setting up boundaries, that these were the rules under which she would meet and I didn't have any say in the matter. I wrote her back and said I would arrive on July fourth and we could meet on the fifth. I would be staying at the Delta South. I got a letter back on June 22 saying she would see me soon.

For the next two weeks, I obsessed about the upcoming trip. Compounding my anxiety about meeting Pat was the fact that my husband, Bob, and I were going through a difficult time. He had lost his job in the fall of 1985 and had just begun a new one. He was under a lot of stress, and spending time with his family was nothing more than an unwelcome distraction from what was important to him—his work. Although he was curious about my search and excited when I finally found Pat, he tended to tune out whenever I slipped into one of my long-winded musings (for which I can't really blame him), and I also kept a lot to myself. So, being left in charge of the children for a weekend was not his idea of fun, but he did grudgingly agree. The kids, luckily, were blissfully unaware of the stress. They were young, eight and ten, and not too interested in what we adults were doing. It was summer and all they cared about was being outside with their friends, so they would hardly even notice that I was gone for two days.

I had never stayed alone in a hotel. I had never even eaten alone in a restaurant. To say that I was very nervous would be a huge understatement. Every nerve in my body was on high alert.

As I checked into the hotel and went to my room on Friday afternoon, I wondered if there would be a message from Pat saying she had changed her mind, but there was no such message. I lay down on the bed for a few minutes and then I got up. I unpacked. Then I lay back down. I looked over at the window and wondered *what now*? I exhausted myself with what ifs. Finally, I went downstairs to dinner. The hotel restaurant was quite large, but the hostess led me to a table for two tucked into a corner, and I was grateful for the privacy it afforded. I think I was twitching the entire time I was there and constantly pushing down my desire to flee.

What I didn't know then was that Pat was there too. She told me the next day that she had come to the hotel that evening and called my room. When there was no answer, she'd gone looking for me in the restaurant but didn't see me at my little corner table—or maybe she just didn't recognize me. I didn't ask her why she'd done that, but I guessed that she might have panicked and needed to get our initial meeting over with as soon as possible, even though she was the one who had set the time.

On Saturday, exactly at noon, there was a knock on my door. When I opened the door, Pat and I looked at each other. I can't remember if we hugged. I don't think so. I stared at her. She was so small. I am not a very big person, but she was tiny. She was dressed in a robin's-egg blue shirt, one button open at the neck. White pants, white shoes— everything crisp. Her hair was brown, not dark but brown, and short. Brown eyes. Not as dark as mine but brown. She was twitchy, almost like a sparrow searching for a place to land. After looking around, she perched on the edge of the bed, one cheek on, one cheek off, ready to jump up again at a moment's notice. It seemed clear to me that she was as close to fleeing as I was. I remember that her hands were in constant motion. Her body language screamed *let's get this over with.* "What do you want to know?" was almost her first question. Not "How are you?" or "My, you look lovely, just like your picture." No niceties. I thought, *Wow, she needs to settle down a bit.* I was very nervous but Pat was vibrating. I sat down next to her and turned to face her.

I said, "Tell me about me."

She began to talk. Her voice was clear, no hesitation.

"I lived in Saskatoon. I was a teacher. I got pregnant and I moved to northern BC to wait for you. I didn't tell anyone why I was leaving. My mother asked me if there was anything I wanted to tell her. I said no. I think she knew, but I couldn't tell her. I won't tell you who your father is. It isn't important right now." (This made it sound as if she might tell me at some point, but, in fact, she never did.) "Towards the time of your birth, I broke my leg. I was taken to Vancouver. I stayed at a home [for unwed mothers] just off Oak Street until you were born. At St. Paul's. After you were born, I stayed with a family that the Sisters introduced me to. You were taken to St. Mary's Hospital. The Sisters took care of you. They would take pictures of you and sneak them to me."

Looking back, I wonder why I didn't ask her more questions about those pictures. How did the nuns get them to her? Had she kept any of them? Thinking about it now, none of that part of her story seems plausible. The Church had strict rules about adoption protocols, and handing out pictures to birth mothers would break all those rules. In the moment, however, I was swept up in her story and afraid that if I interrupted her to ask for clarification, she would just stop talking altogether. It was years later when I began to doubt the truth behind her story. There was a bit of a fairy-tale quality to her words that day and I was a sucker for a fairy-tale. I wanted to believe everything she said. After all, one of my big wishes had come true. She was sitting in front of me, she was real!

Finally, she took a breath. I think she'd been talking without breathing. I was hardly breathing either. The first time I asked my parents why I had to stay in the orphanage for three months, they told me I had something wrong with my legs and had to be in a cast. That turned out to be completely false, and years later they told me the truth. I couldn't be adopted right after I was born in September because my birth mother didn't sign the final papers until December. three months after I was born. Now I asked Pat why she had waited so long.

"It was very hard for me," she said. "I looked at the pictures the Sisters gave me and I couldn't do anything. I couldn't see you, hold you. I couldn't do anything for you. For me."

For me? It was an odd, incomplete sentence, but she stumbled a number of times while telling her story, as if she were searching for the right words to complete her thoughts. As I watched her, it seemed as if she was not just telling me about that time in her life but allowing herself to slip back into it. I held my breath a little bit longer, hoping that if I was silent, she might linger with her memories. If she wanted to.

She never told me how the nuns got those pictures to her or the whole story about why she waited three months to sign the adoption papers. But at that first meeting, I had much more important questions on my mind. I wanted to know how she'd met my father, whether he had been a special person in her life, and whether he knew about me.

I told you, I won't talk about your father. She hadn't told before that day because I hadn't asked in in my letters. I had wanted to but was never brave enough. Perhaps she thought I had or perhaps she had been practising her answer—who knows. But, when I finally did ask who my father was, that was her answer, and for the next thirty years, she repeated that sentence every time I asked her about my father.

Instead, she went back to talking about why she had finally decided to sign the adoption papers. "I finally made the decision. I had to sign the papers. I couldn't look after you on my own. A single woman, Catholic. I couldn't teach as an unwed mother, and so I would have no means of support."

I knew this was true. In the eyes of the Catholic church, having a child out of wedlock was a sin. If the Church knew about it, Pat would not be hired to work in any Catholic-run workplace, including schools, even after the birth. And Pat's situation was complicated even further by the fact that my birth father would have to get a divorce to marry her, which was yet another sin. You couldn't marry a divorced person and continue to receive the sacraments. In fact, if she kept me and married a divorced man, she might be excommunicated.

"So, I signed. Then I left Vancouver and moved across the country, as far away from you as I could get. I had to go. Then I met George. He wasn't Catholic, but I married him anyway. I wanted children. I wanted a family. We moved to Calgary, where the girls were born. And here we are. Still."

I thought it was peculiar that she would marry a non-Catholic. Pat had a very strong Catholic faith and with that faith came lots of rules! Many dos and don'ts. Marrying a divorced non-Catholic was probably in the top three of the 'don'ts'— the combination that apparently eliminated my birth father from the running. Marrying a non-Catholic was almost as troublesome. I suspect it would have been in the top five 'don'ts' in those days. But not an excommunicable offense. Perhaps Pat was getting frightened, worried that she might never get married and have the long wished for family. I don't really know. But George wasn't divorced, and he agreed that they would raise their children in the Catholic faith, which apparently made the choice acceptable to her.

Hearing her say that it had been difficult to give me up was comforting, but I wasn't sure she was being entirely truthful. Maybe she was just saying it to make me feel better. Later in our relationship, as I got to know her better, I did come to believe her, but in that moment, sitting in that hotel room, I felt as if I were on the verge of tears, and I didn't want to cry. I had to step away from our conversation. The intensity was overwhelming, so I stood. Pat stopped talking and looked at me, startled, as if she had forgotten where she was or who she was talking to. I knew she'd been turning over memories that had been locked away for years. She was saying words out loud that she had never said to anyone else, and she looked frightened.

We both needed a break. I reached over and touched her hand. "Let's go out," I said. "Enough talking for now." We stepped into the sunshine and the world looked the same as it had an hour earlier, except it wasn't. It was completely changed—for me and for Pat. The gossamer-like thread that bound us in the moment of birth had begun to re-emerge. Even that short, stilted conversation had been a beginning, a renewal.

We left the hotel and spent the rest of the afternoon wandering in a shopping center. We stopped for lunch, did some window shopping, chatting as we walked— trivial conversation. But that was okay. It was all we could manage. We said goodbye in the late afternoon with a promise to get together again the next day.

Back in my room, I sank into a chair by the window. There wasn't much of a view but I didn't care; all I saw was Pat's face. I sat there for a long time, trying to figure out what I was feeling. Part of me was numb. Pat's words were ricocheting off one another in my brain as I struggled to recall exactly what she had said. I wished I'd recorded all of it so I would have her words forever. I thought of more questions and lined them up in my mind, ready for the next day. My final thought was a good one, and it actually surprised me: I liked Pat.

We met for lunch on Sunday, and this time there was less tension between us. But I still had one more big question I couldn't go home without asking: "Tell me why you named Kim, Kim." I needed to know why she had named two daughters Kim. I had asked her that question in one of my letters, but all she said was, "a second Kim could never really take the place of a first Kim. Weird eh?" Now, as we sat across from one another and I asked her again, she looked past me and then directly at me. Her vibrating body quieted slightly; even her hands were still. "I gave the love for two to one." What did that mean? For a moment, I was happy because she had answered my question. But in the next moment, I was angry and hurt. Her answer was ridiculous. I felt betrayed. I raged in my head. *You left me, but at least you gave me a name before you went. Only then you gave it to someone else. My name was not available for you to give to another child. How dare you!* But then a crazy thing happened. I started to laugh. I looked at her and said, "Are you kidding me? There are thousands of names out there and you give the same one to two of us?" I couldn't make sense of what she had said. It felt more like an excuse than the truth. And then I wondered if perhaps it had been her only way to survive. If she had one Kim with her maybe she could live without the other Kim. Maybe. She looked at me and smiled but didn't say any more about the name. She never ever said anything more about the name. I guess she thought her answer had satisfied me.

As the years passed, I realized that, in an odd way, the conversations we had during that first meeting were among the more honest exchanges we ever had. Pat was such a secretive person, always on guard, so afraid to say too much for fear of opening herself up to questions she wasn't prepared to answer, that I believe her giving the briefest possible responses to any questions was her way of being as honest as she could be. I sensed her reluctance to break her own code of silence. It was as if when she signed the adoption papers, she had made a pact with herself to say nothing ever again about the circumstances of her life in 1951 and 1952—how she met my father, the nature of their relationship, my birth, giving me up. And, at no time on that weekend in Calgary did she give me one moment of hope that she would ever break her silence. No one in her life would ever know about me. It was years later, in a letter, that she said she would tell her daughters about me. But only if her husband George was dead. On that weekend in 1986, I saw no hope of ever finding out who my father was or of meeting my sisters. Shame settled on my shoulders and the invisible chain rattled. Not worthy.

At that first lunch, however, I still wanted her to confide in me, trust me the way a daughter could be trusted. I asked her to tell me more about herself, and she answered a few of my questions about her early life. She told me her parents were divorced when she was about ten and that she had practically raised her brother and sister because her mother had to work. She told me about becoming a teacher and her love of teaching English and drama. She also talked about being asked to host a radio show that focused on the arts and culture community. She became quite animated when she talked about that work, but she didn't go into very much detail. She talked a little about her three daughters, but as with many of the topics we touched on, she was stingy with specifics.

After lunch, she drove me to the airport, and when we arrived, she turned to me and smiled, handing me a card. Then she stretched across the space between us, hugged me, and said, "Thank you for coming." At the entrance to the terminal, I looked back over my shoulder. She was standing by the side of her car. She lifted her hand and waved. I wondered if I would ever see her again.

Once I was inside, I opened her card. It said: *You are in Big Trouble…I have decided I like You.* She signed it: *Thank you Kim, Pat*

On the plane, I closed my eyes and let my mind roam free. There had been moments of joy in our meeting, but it was clouded by sadness. Why had I opened this door? What was the point? I was once more overwhelmed by those old feelings of rejection. Pat couldn't or wouldn't bring me into the open and tell the world about me as I'd hoped she would. She had a life—a husband and three daughters. I was the mistake. So what if she liked me? I was still a big, fat secret.

As my plane landed, I did what I always did with feelings I couldn't make sense of; I tucked them away, letting them rest. I was surprised to see my family waiting for me at the airport. The children knew I was adopted but didn't know that I had gone to meet my birth mother. I told them I was going to Calgary to see a friend. They asked if I'd had a nice visit with my friend and I told them we had a lovely time, then deflected any further questions by asking them what they had done while I was away.

Driving home, I gave Bob the short version of what happened. I spoke quietly, and the children, chattering to each other in the back seat, couldn't have been less interested in what the grownups were talking about. I said it had gone better than I expected. Overall it was good, great even. Meeting Pat had been a lifelong dream. I wished she had shared more information with me, but still, for a first visit it was good. He asked a few questions about what Pat was like and I kept my answers light. When we got home, he disappeared into his workshop, which was a good thing because I didn't want to talk about the weekend anymore. Not with him, not with anyone.

My friends Anne and Leah knew I was going to meet my birth mother but I hadn't told anyone else, not my parents or my brothers. My parents (particularly my mother) didn't really want to hear about anything to do with my search. Verd, I believe, would have listened and tried to help if I'd asked him, but I didn't. And Dan knew absolutely nothing about what I was doing. Thinking about it now, I believe my need for secrecy both fed into and was fed by my shame. Meeting Pat did nothing to alleviate that feeling.

Chapter Six

Life Goes On

The letters resumed. In an odd way, it was as if we had never met face to face. Over the next three years, we traded stories about our day-to-day lives, nothing of any great significance. Pat was teaching at a special school that focused on the arts. She would tell me stories about the kids who attended the school and about the art festivals she was preparing for. Her three girls were now young women, and she touched briefly on the ups and downs they encountered as they made their way in the world. Her letters were cheerful, often four or five pages long, but she rarely said anything about how she was feeling about our relationship. Each time I received a letter, I hoped it would have a sentence at the end saying how glad she was that we were in touch. And I was always disappointed. Looking back, I should have realized that just by answering my letters, she was telling me she was glad I was back in her life. But I didn't know her very well at this point, and in many ways, I was less mature than I realized. I could easily slip back into a childlike desire for her to spell out her love. So, our correspondence continued to be light and breezy. It was as if we were on the world's longest first date. I wondered if we would ever have deeper conversations.

In 1988, I was offered the position of Director of Volunteer Services at BC's Children's Hospital in Vancouver. It was a dream job for me. Hundreds of people came to the hospital every year wishing to volunteer with the children. It was my job to make sure they had the qualifications to work with our patients. I was the main interface between the hospital and the community. I loved every minute of my work and I was excited to share this news with Pat. But, at the same time, I was growing frustrated with the cheerful, newsy letters we'd been exchanging. I decided it was time for another face-to-face meeting.

In the summer of 1989, I offered to fly to Calgary again, and she agreed to meet with me. I was hoping that this time I could get her to tell me more about herself, about my father, and perhaps about her relationship with him (even though she had been clear that she was never going to tell me any of that). I also wanted to talk to her about her three daughters, find out when she would tell them about me. Deep in my heart I wondered if she would ever tell them but I kept pushing that little detail down. Ever the optimist!

As it turned out, this visit was nothing like the previous one. I thought I was booking myself into the same hotel I'd stayed in before, but it turned out to be a sister hotel. They were next door to each other but as different as night and day. This hotel was old, and the room smelled musty, which just increased the discomfort and anxiety I was already feeling. I should have asked to move to the other hotel, but Pat was coming to this one, and I had no way to contact her because phone calls to her house wcrc strictly forbidden. I could have left a message with the front desk. I could have done lots of things, but I didn't. I stayed.

Once again Pat knocked on the door at the exact time we'd agreed to meet, but it was immediately clear that she was uneasy. The first time we met, she was nervous but also excited. This time she looked stiff and brittle. No chitchat on the edge of the bed this time. I asked her if she wanted to go out to lunch and when she nodded, I picked up my handbag and we left. There was a chill in the air around us and I wondered what the day would bring. It was years later before I found out that I was just one of many 'challenges' on her plate at that time. Her husband was unwell and her three daughters were each having their own life challenges. She said nothing about any of this to me so I did what I always did—made it all about me!

We sat across from each other at lunch and caught up on what had been happening in our lives. What were my kids up to? How was my work going? What was she doing now that she had retired? How was George feeling? What were each of her girls doing? I gave a small sigh of relief and thought that maybe this would be okay after all. I ignored the prickliness that radiated from Pat. I came to regretted that misstep. I took a breath and then I asked the big question—the one I'd come to ask. "Tell me more about you and my father." Clearly, that was the wrong approach! I should have eased into it; I should have said something like, "I know this is hard for you, but, please, will you tell me about my father?" Instead, I leapt straight in. Luckily, I didn't broach the subject until we had finished eating, because that question brought lunch to an abrupt halt. Pat's response was to stare at me in silent rage for a long moment. You couldn't miss the anger. She sat up very straight and carefully placed her fork on the table and then she looked at me. Those brown eyes snapped as if an electric current was passing through them. It was her turn to take a big breath. And then she spoke. "I told you before, I will not answer questions about your father. Ever. And I have told you all that you need to know about my past. If you can't accept that, we have nothing more to talk about. I would like to take you back to your hotel now."

I was stunned. What had just happened? She stood up and started to walk away. I put some money on the table and caught up with her at the door. We moved together to the car and drove in silence back to the hotel. Then she turned and said cheerfully. "I'll pick you up for lunch tomorrow."

I was still reeling from her response to my question, to the anger that radiated from her in the restaurant, and here she was acting as if that whole exchange had never happened. It was bizarre.

I got out of the car, went to my room, and collapsed on the bed in tears. I raged at her, at myself. What did I think would happen when I asked that question? Even if I had eased into it, danced around it for a bit, I think that both her response and my feelings would have been the same. The familiar slide began—I was given away, I wasn't wanted, I was worthless. Hours passed, evening light faded to black. I faded to black.

I woke up the next morning knowing that I needed to leave. That old reliable flight pattern was back in force. I packed, checked out, and waited for Pat to arrive. She thought we were having lunch but I asked her to drive me to the airport instead. She didn't ask why and I offered no explanation. Her words and actions had hurt and bewildered me, and I was all out of courage; instead of asking why she had acted the way she did, I ran away. At the airport, she said goodbye. No hug this time; no card either. I closed the car door and walked away. I didn't look back. I was empty, confused, and sad. The sadness wrapped around my heart and squeezed. It was hard to breathe.

Much to my relief, no one was waiting for me at the airport this time. I made my own way home praying that everyone would be out. I was in luck; the house was empty. I sat on the front porch and wondered *now what?*

When the kids did arrive, unlike the last time I visited Pat, they were full of questions. They were now three years older and more curious. This time they knew I was meeting with my birth mother, and they wanted to know what she was like. Any other time, I might have welcomed their questions but not that day. All I could say was, "She was nice," without expanding on that simple statement. Luckily, when they realized there weren't going to be any juicy details, they lost interest and wandered away.

Bob pressed me for more, but I just shrugged. "I remember the last trip was good." he said. "It was tough this time," I replied. "How?" he asked. I didn't know what to say, so I shrugged again, and as I turned away, I said, "I can't explain it right now. Maybe later." He didn't ask any more questions, and I did something unheard of. It was four o'clock on Sunday afternoon and I went to bed. I couldn't think straight. I had no easy, lighthearted answers to my family's questions, and because I had kept my feelings about my adoption private for so long, talking about how I was feeling now was just too hard.

The next day I had to go to work. I was responsible for an all-day meeting that couldn't be postponed, so I dragged myself out of bed and headed to the hospital. No one at work knew I was adopted. I'd kept that part of my life a secret. Therefore, no one asked me any questions. I did what I had to do for the day, and when it was over, I crawled back into bed and stayed there for three days. My husband had left on a business trip that morning so he wasn't around to ask what was wrong. I told the kids I must have caught a bug on the plane. Thankfully, they accepted my explanation and left me alone, because I had nothing to give—them or anyone else. What had happened to me? I had no words to describe my feelings because I didn't know what I was feeling. The hollowness inside me defied explanation. But eventually, of necessity, I rejoined life and went to work.

When I walked back into the hospital, the first person I saw was the Director of Psychology. I grabbed her by the arm and dragged her into my office, slammed the door, and tearfully spilled the whole story, including what had happened the previous weekend. I had never spoken to any kind of healthcare professional about my adoption, so it felt serendipitous that the first person I encountered that morning was a psychologist. It helped that she was also a trusted friend. She listened and then took my hands. Gently but firmly she said, "You have been wrestling with demons all your life. Your mother left you when you were a baby. Whatever her reasons, the fact remains, she left. You fought back, but these connections we have with each other, mother and child, these are the deepest, most basic in our lives. When they are disrupted, your axis is out of kilter. How can you possibly know what to feel or what to think? You had built great hope over these last few years that your mother would somehow want to redeem herself and make everything right for you. It seems like this weekend shattered that hope. I think it must have felt like she rejected you all over again. That's what you saw, what you felt. It may have been very different for her. You don't know what she was feeling. But right now, we are talking about you, not her. What do you do now? Walking back through the weekend and making sense of it will take time. To look at those hopes, those dreams you have been holding, and decide, what now? That will take lots of time. You will need to be kind to yourself. And to her. Can you do that?"

I didn't know if I could figure it out by myself. Maybe I did need someone to be a dispassionate listener, someone who would challenge my assumptions and point to new pathways. I just didn't know.

My friend and colleague sat with me for a long time that morning. Our conversation helped me to understand that I had choices to make, but first I would have to figure out what I really wanted. Did I want to stay connected to Pat? At any cost? Or did I want to cut my losses and walk away? I just didn't know. She checked in with me a few times after that, but I kept our conversations short and light. After a few tries, she left me alone, and I went back to my solitary pursuit of what I had begun to think of as 'Life with Pat.' It seemed to me that I had to do this on my own. Asking for help would mean opening up and sharing my feelings of abandonment and rejection, what it felt like to be someone's secret. And, for better or worse, I simply didn't want to do that. Anne and Leah had helped me with the practical aspects of my search but I kept a tight hold on the emotional turmoil I felt about my adoption. I replayed my friend's words and one particular phrase stuck with me, "…when they [connections between mother and child] are disrupted, your axis is out of kilter." I thought, maybe that's what I am trying to do—rebalance myself, hoping that my renewed relationship with Pat would wash away the years of feeling rejected and ashamed. But that same shame stopped me from asking for help.

On the plane ride home that sunny day in 1989 I had struggled to find the words to describe the deep loss I felt. It was as if there had been a death that weekend as significant as any I'd experienced up to that point in my life. It was the death of my dream that Pat would acknowledge me to the world. Not only was she not willing to tell anyone about me, she wasn't even willing to tell me about my father. I had to find a way to let go of my anger about her choices.

Our relationship changed after that weekend, although I'm not sure what happened for Pat, because she never said and I never asked. Once again, courage eluded me. Months passed before either of us wrote again, but finally, I sent her a card with a note saying, "Hello, hope all is well." She responded quickly with a short newsy letter—nothing of much significance, but it was enough to get us started again.

In those intervening months, I'd thought a lot about the relationship we had created. It was based mainly on the present. We had been sharing the ups and downs of our current lives, but I couldn't get her to answer any questions about my conception. Now I had a choice to make. I could stop writing and give her up altogether or I could accept her boundaries and continue to write about the here and now. I chose the latter. I knew I could easily slip back into hopefulness, wishing on a star for her to want more of our relationship. But in my heart, I knew that was never going to happen. And yet I couldn't let her slip away completely. In an unspoken pact, I agreed to remain her secret.

So, she kept writing and I kept answering. And I also had an ulterior motive. I had three sisters and I wanted to keep every possible avenue open so that perhaps, one day, I could meet them. Over time, I had begun to doubt her earlier promise to eventually tell them about me, but I wasn't ready to give up. My sisters were out there and I wanted to know them.

In 1991, my husband's work situation changed again and we found ourselves on the way to Hong Kong. I was sad to leave my hospital job but this opportunity was too good to pass up. It was exciting and terrifying. The kids, who were both teenagers by then, weren't too happy, but we went anyway, and slowly even they adjusted to our new life. The kind of work I had been doing at the hospital in Vancouver didn't exist in Hong Kong so I went back to teaching. I taught first grade at the Canadian International School, which gave me lots to share with Pat. Once again, we found common ground and our letters found a new lease on life. I looked forward to reading hers in a way I hadn't before. Perhaps it was because I was so far from home and letters were an important connection to the part of my life I'd left behind. Perhaps I was finally accepting that I wasn't going to get everything I wanted from Pat. The soul-searching I had done after that catastrophic weekend in

1989 taught me a few critical lessons: I needed to stop expecting Pat to be someone she couldn't be for me and I needed to accept the boundaries she needed created around what we discussed. I also needed to acknowledge that I had no idea what Pat's life was like, what problems she may have been dealing with and that this situation wasn't all about me. It seemed that it took a move to the other side of the world for me to recognize that perhaps Pat was giving as much as she could. My sharing school trivia and stories about life in Hong Kong would have to be enough for now, for both of us. Meanwhile she shared stories that often revolved around my three sisters. For whatever reason, sharing those bits of information about my sisters was within her boundaries, and I loved hearing about them.

On my return to Vancouver in 1994, I resumed my work as a Director for Volunteer Services but this time at St. Paul's hospital, where I was born. It was the same kind of work I had done at BC Children's hospital but on a much larger scale within a very complex system. AIDS was raging in our city and St. Paul's was the center of care for these patients. It was a busy and challenging job.

Business took me to Calgary three times between 1994 and 2000. Pat and I would meet but our visits were always short, usually just coffee or tea in a hotel restaurant. Light conversation was all we could manage. We never touched the tough stuff again. I always left her with an ache in my heart, but I was, nevertheless, grateful even for those quick meetings. I wanted her to know that I was doing well, that my children were thriving, that she could be proud of me. And then, I would get angry with myself for craving her approval. It was exhausting.

Over the next fifteen years, the time between visits grew longer, as did the time between letters. Pat's life appeared to be very chaotic. She alluded to ill health, hers and George's, but gave few details. She wrote about what the girls were doing—finishing school, having babies. Miji had two sons and so did Kim. Later, Robin joined in with two sons of her own. Somewhere in the midst of that time, both Miji and Kim divorced and remarried. All three girls had gone to university and studied education. According to Pat, Robin and Miji were teaching but Kim wasn't. There were no other details. Our letters were, in effect, a series of headlines with very little follow-up.

In May 2006, George died, and in 2009 Pat moved to a senior living facility. After he died, her letters were few and far between, but they kept coming. And, in spite of myself, I still kept hoping she would surprise me with the answers to the questions I had asked years before about my father. And I hoped that she would tell my sisters about me. But even as she advanced in age, Pat showed no interest in telling me about my father or disclosing my existence to her daughters. It was discouraging because time was slipping away.

During these same years, my life was also pretty chaotic. My marriage had been strained to the breaking point when we lived in Hong Kong, and I had hoped that it would improve once we got home. But over the next year things just went from bad to worse. Bob had been let go from his job in Asia, leaving him with a very bruised ego. He was angry about what had happened to him and he turned his frustration on me. Although he'd always had a tendency to be verbally offensive, the tirades became more frequent and more intense. I never knew what his mood would be when I got home from work, and I felt as if I were constantly walking on egg shells. The atmosphere in the house had been charged with anger for too long. It was time for it to stop.

Bob was a complicated man. Our marriage had many good moments and the joy of bringing two children into the world topped the list. Shawna and Matthew were our joy. But, at the end of the day, our differences overtook us and it left a divide too wide to close.

Finally, I'd had enough, and on April 1, 1995, I moved out. My children were then sixteen and nineteen years old. I told them I was leaving and that they could come with me or stay with their dad; they were welcome in both places. They chose to come with me but visited regularly with Bob. I rented a semidetached house that we fondly referred to as the dump. It was not anything like the beautiful house I had left, but it ended up being more of a home than I'd had for a long time. It was a peaceful place, filled with laughter. The separation from my husband was fraught with drama, but I did my best to leave the drama outside the door. Bob came over a couple of times to bring the kids back after a visit or to 'check in' with me. But I didn't want him in this new space, so I asked him not to visit. He wasn't happy about that, but he didn't fight me on it either. The house became my safe haven.

My dad died of lung cancer that same year at the age of 74. It was only seven months from diagnosis to death. It was a shock even though we knew his illness was terminal. He had been the epicenter of our world and his loss was devastating. My mother wasn't coping very well so my brothers put her on a plane to me and she stayed for six weeks. During that time t she made the decision to move permanently from Ontario to British Columbia. She lived with me for the next seventeen years, until she went into an assisted living facility. Shawna married in 1997 and had a son, Cameron, in 2000. Matthew travelled to Australia in 1998 and on his return in 2000 met his soon-to-be wife, Jennifer. I went back to school in 1999, got my Master's degree in leadership, and in 2002 I began teaching leadership, organizational behavior, and research courses at the School of Applied Sciences and the Faculty of Management at Royal Roads University in Victoria. At the same time, I started a private consulting practice that focused on strategic planning, team development, conflict resolution, and coaching. Between teaching and consulting, life was busy. It was also filled with unexpected joy, because, the same year I began teaching at Royal Roads University, I met Chad, the man who would become my second husband.

In the spring of 2006, my daughter's then five-year-old son Cameron, was diagnosed with a brain tumor. It was a horrific time for our family but we had a lot of support, sometimes from surprising sources. H.Y. Louie, the grocery store chain and wholesale distribution company my son-in-law Jim, worked for, championed Cameron's fight by fundraising for BC Children's Hospital. One of the ways they did this was to create a teddy bear, which they named Cameron Bear, to sell in their stores. I told Pat about Cameron whenever I wrote, and in her letters, she always asked how my grandson was doing. I sent her a bear for Christmas the year they became available. It was a bit odd to send an 84-year-old woman a stuffed bear, but I sent them to all the important people in my life that Christmas, and she was one of them. I'm happy to say that Cameron survived his ordeal and, as I am writing this, is about to graduate from high school.

The last time I visited Pat was in 2010. I was going to Calgary on business for the university where I was teaching, so I wrote and asked if we could meet. She invited me to visit her at the facility where she was living, which was surprising because up until then we had always met on neutral ground. But Pat was no longer able to drive, and I like to think that perhaps her wish to see me outweighed her need to keep me out of her personal space. As I approached the residence, just knowing that I was about to see her triggered those old familiar emotions—rejection, shame, and abandonment. They swirled like a gentle fog, moving in the space between heart and mind. A chill grew inside of me and I became more anxious with each step. And, it had been so many years since we last met that I wondered if I would even recognize her. I pushed open the door and entered a large, light, beautifully furnished sitting room filled with old folks, some with eyes closed and heads resting on their chests, some sitting upright and staring straight ahead, but without any light in their eyes. On the other hand, there were also those whose eyes lit up at the sight of a new person coming to visit. I checked at the desk and was told that Pat was out, so I wandered around the sitting area, smiling, touching a hand here and there. I wondered where Pat was and hoped she hadn't forgotten we were meeting. In the same moment, my old nemesis 'flight' crashed through my body and all I wanted to do was flee. It would have been so easy—just turn and walk. But just then the front door flew open and a tiny, energetic lady came plowing through, pushing a walker. She was dressed beautifully in black pants, a black jacket with a red rose pinned to the lapel, and a crisp white shirt with the collar standing up just so. Pat was back and she was beaming at me. In that instant, my heart was full and I wondered if today were the day she would say she was sorry for not choosing me. In an instant, all my hopes and dreams collided in that room filled with old people.

She hugged me, smiling, then pushed her walker ahead of me, talking all the way. As she walked, she told me that she was just returning from an award ceremony at Catholic Family Services of Calgary. They had named an award in her honour for outstanding volunteer contribution. That was where she got the rose. She told me that she had begun volunteering for the organization shortly after our initial meeting in 1986. Her focus was on helping unwed mothers decide whether to keep their babies or give them up for adoption and how to move forward with their lives once the baby was born. I was stunned. She had never mentioned anything about this to me, and I had to wonder whether she had shared the secret of my birth with any of those women. If so, as far as I knew, they would be the only ones she had ever told.

While I pondered the implications of what she was saying, she chattered on, describing her new home as we made our way to her suite. She laughed as she described the exercise classes she took, telling me they helped her strike back at the aging process. She was acting as if my being there were perfectly normal. We took twists and turns though the maze of hallways and finally arrived at suite number 52. I'd sent lots of mail to that address. Inside the tiny apartment, the first thing I saw was a crucifix hanging on the wall in the hallway, her deep faith ever-present. The air smelled clean, with a hint of her signature perfume, Channel No.5. Looking left toward the living room, I saw a crowded but bright space filled with colonial-style furniture, a big desk, and lots of books everywhere.

In the short hallway leading to the living room Pat had hung several photographs. One picture was of the three girls when they were little, individual photos framed as one collage. As I stopped to look at them, I was surprised to see one of them was of my eight-year-old self. How did Pat even have that? Pat was still talking as she settled herself into a chair, but I was in shock. Instantly, I realized that it wasn't me; it was the other Kim. She looked just like me at that age: same ridiculous glasses, same funny haircut. I leaned in for a closer look. Big eyes looked back at me. The picture was black and white but I could see that her eyes were light colored while mine were dark but still! Unbelievable. Slowly, my feet moved. They took the rest of my body with them, but my mind lingered on the pictures. I sat and Pat chattered. I kept sneaking peeks over my shoulder. The picture was still there, still looked like me, but wasn't me. And for a moment I was flooded with a sense of loss for all that might have been.

Pat said my name and I jerked back into the reality of the moment. *Focus*! She was talking about her life and how difficult it had been to make the move to this place. Then she pointed to a basket in the corner that was full of the teddy bears, including a little one dressed in a grey sweatshirt. Cameron Bear was sitting amidst about a dozen or so others. When I sent it to her, I'd had no idea she collected teddy bears, but when I asked her about it that day, she told me she'd been collecting them for years. She said she couldn't bring all the bears with her when she moved, so only her favorites had made the trip. I wondered if having Cameron Bear as part of her collection allowed her to keep me close in a way that was manageable for her. I didn't ask and she didn't say. I simply made up my own story—as usual! When it was time to leave, I hugged her and she hugged back, each of us, it seemed, reluctant to let go. As I began to drive away, I turned and waved. She was standing outside the door clutching her walker, the wind lifting her wispy hair. Her fingers fluttered, a small wave, just like at the airport in 1986. I snuck a final peak and she was still there, watching me. It was the last time I saw her.

Given her advancing age, I'd developed the habit of checking the obituaries in the Calgary paper if I hadn't heard from Pat for a few months. It was a bit macabre but it was all I could do. Back in 1985 she had promised to make sure someone let me know when she died, but as the years passed and I understood her better, I came to realize that there was no way she would to do that. Asking someone to contact me meant the someone would know I existed and might start asking questions about the nature of my relationship with Pat. So I checked the paper from time to time. Her last letter to me was dated January 29, 2015. She did not respond to a letter I sent in the early spring, and when I logged onto to obituary section of the paper on June 4 and typed her name into the search box, as I had done four or five times before, she was listed. She had died on April

29, 2015. She was 92. I don't know why my last letter to her wasn't returned to me.

I am not sure why I checked the paper on that particular day. Perhaps because my dog had died that morning and I thought that, if Pat's name appeared, I could get all the sorrow out in one day. There was no logic at work here, but when I saw her name, I was overcome by such profound sadness that I could hardly breathe. When I told my children, Matthew said, "Mum, it must be so hard to grieve anonymously." I frantically scanned my memory. What was I doing on April 29? How come I didn't feel her passing? In all the romance novels I had read and the sappy TV shows I had watched over the years, the absent child always seemed to 'feel' her mother's passing, but not me. In some peculiar way, I thought that if I were doing something worthwhile, I would be forgiven for not knowing. In fact, I was doing something important— attending a memorial service for a colleague. I told myself, that counts. Right?

When Pat died, she took with her the answers to so many questions and the potential fulfillment of so many wishes. The loss I felt for something I'd never had was astounding. How could I feel this way when my brain had told me for years that I had no right to feel much of anything? But in that moment, no matter what my brain had been telling me, my heart was broken— because she was gone, because I had three sisters who didn't even know I existed and because she had kept me a secret until the end. The shame attached to my existence endured for her entire lifetime. I was sixty-three years old and still her secret.

Chapter Seven
Saying Goodbye to My Father

On my birth certificate, the space for my father's name is blank and it remains blank. When Pat died, my hopes of learning anything about my father died too.

Years earlier, my husband, Chad, asked me why I had searched for my mother and not my father. But I had searched for both. In fact, when I received the non-identifying information from the government, I started the search for my father first, because there were a few clues that I hoped would make it easier than trying to find my mother. I am not sure why I thought that, because, frankly, the information was vague.

The social worker wrote: "He was 40 yrs. old at the time of your birth and of Irish racial origin. He had a doctorate and was a university professor. He was six feet tall, with a heavy build, brown hair and eyes, and had an outgoing personality. His health and that of his family was said to be good. His main interest was sports." That description created the bare outlines of a picture in my mind.

A tiny bit of ambiguous information and a ton of assumptions guided my search. He was a professor. Since my mother was living in Saskatoon when I was conceived,

I figured that my father must have been working in Saskatoon as well, and there was only one university in Saskatoon. I scoured the year books at the University of Saskatchewan looking for a face that resembled mine. He was ten years older than Pat, so I looked for an older man. Lots of dark haired, dark eyed men looked back at me, but the pictures were black and white, making everyone appear to have dark hair and dark eyes, and they all looked old. Asking every dark-haired man of a certain age in Saskatoon if he were my father didn't seem like a very good plan. So I decided to refocus on looking for my birth mother.

At that point, I still foolishly assumed that if and when I did find my birth mother, she would tell me about my father. But, as it turned out, Pat not only steadfastly refused to talk about him, she wouldn't even confirm that the information she had given the social worker was accurate. Still, I always wondered if he had known about me and if I were his secret as well as hers. Now, with Pat gone, it was time to say a final goodbye to him too, so I decided to write him a letter of farewell.

Dear Father, Dad, Sir (Or should I just say Hello? Hi?)

My name is Kim and I was born September 12, 1952. I am your daughter. I think you know about me—maybe. Do you remember Pat? Pat Murphy? Pat has been very secretive about you. She wouldn't tell me who you were, leaving me to wonder, speculate about you.

I was adopted by a good family. My parents loved me very much. I did well in school, at least well enough to go to university. I studied mathematics in university. It was not my intended goal, it just emerged. I thought that I should study a hard subject so I picked mathematics. It was hard for me! Eventually I returned to school for my Master's degree and like you, I now teach at a university. At least I think you did! I have often wondered if the little information that I do have about you is actually true or if Pat made up a story just to satisfy the social worker at the time of my birth. I will never know for sure will.

Despite the love I was given as a child, there was a void. The yearning to know about you and my mother was strong. I thought about you and I wondered, where are you? Did you know about me? And if you did know about me, why didn't you fight to keep me? Maybe you didn't know there was a me. Or maybe fighting for me wasn't what you wanted to do.

The social worker's letter implied that you knew Pat was pregnant, but there was nothing to say what you wanted to happen with me. Ultimately, it seems to me that Pat, alone, decided what would happen with me. Despite her careful planning, life as she knew it was over when she became pregnant. She went on to craft a new life. Neither you nor I was part of that life. What did you know about her plans? What did you say? On December 21, 1952, I was placed in the arms of my new parents. Did you talk to her after that day?

I wanted to meet you. I thought about you often and I looked for you. I visited Saskatoon a few times as an adult and I always looked at the older men who walked by me, wondering if you were one of them. A bit creepy but good intentioned! When Pat died, any hope of finding you died too. But I think about you often, still.

Your daughter, Kim

As I reread my letter, I realized once again how memories can shift, creating new stories that may or may not be accurate. Pat's extreme reaction the first time I asked her face-to-face about my father kept me from ever doing that again. I did try asking her in letters, but, to be honest, I'm not sure I even sent them. I wrote many letters to her that ultimately ended up in the trash because I was afraid of what her reaction might be. Even as I write this, I can still remember her fury with me that day at lunch when I asked about my father. I didn't want that to happen again so I simply didn't ask. Basically, I was a coward.

Shame is a funny thing, and I wondered if Pat's shame about her pregnancy stopped her from telling me who my father was and what he had meant to her. Was he just some random guy she had sex with or did she have an ongoing relationship with him? I didn't really think this was the case given he apparently said he would get a divorce to marry her but her secrecy left me wondering where truth stopped and started with her. But Pat's adamant refusal to answer those questions didn't stop me from thinking about him and wondering *what if.*

In the end, writing to my father was my way of saying goodbye and finally letting go of my long-held hopes and wishes. My dad's words echoed in my head, *"You may not find what you want, you may not get everything you wish for."* As I finished writing that letter, I said a silent prayer, wishing both him and Pat peace in their final resting places.

Chapter Eight
Getting Permission from Pat

I had promised Pat that I would never contact Kim, Robin or Miji without her permission. She had said she would tell them "one day"—but not until after George died. Then he died, but she still didn't tell them. I don't think she could. I believe that the older she got, the less able she was to confront the ghost of her shame. Her secret was so deeply imbedded in her bones that to tell the girls would have caused her more pain than giving me away. But once she was gone, I wondered if I was still obliged to remain hidden. Was it time to find my three sisters?

I wrestled with this question for a couple of months. I had asked her only once, early in our relationship, if she would tell them. But because she didn't, I had to figure out what I was going to do now.

I taught an ethics class as part of my organizational behavior course, so I was used to discussing the challenges of making good decisions in difficult situations. In the classroom, however, those challenges were academic—to be discussed and debated. Facing my own personal dilemma was an entirely different matter. As the instructor, it was easy to explore the pros and cons of real dilemmas the students were currently dealing with or ones they wanted to revisit from their past, and help them decide what to do or what they might have done. It wasn't so easy when the issue was my own.

Twice before, when I was at a crossroad in my life, I had consulted a psychic, and each time, what the psychic told me about my future had turned out to be true. The first one was a man who had set up a table on a street corner. Ordinarily, I would just have walked past him, but on a whim, I stopped and sat down. He smiled and said hello, took my ten dollars, and fanned out a deck of Tarot cards. He studied them in silence for a few minutes while I wondered why I had sat down. Then he began to speak, He told me I was going to teach at a small university and live in a house in the trees. His predictions seemed farfetched at the time, but I thanked him anyway, got up, and kept walking.

The second time I was more purposeful in seeking advice. My marriage had collapsed, my father had recently died, and I was adrift. A friend had told me about a psychic named Gloria, so I made an appointment. When I knocked on her door, a very tiny but otherwise ordinary looking woman answered. She welcomed me in and offered me a chair. To be honest, I was a bit disappointed. I'd hoped she would have a scarf wrapped around her head and speak with a Transylvanian accent. But what she said was anything but ordinary. She told me that I needed music in my life and I should play the harp. Given my complete lack of musical talent, that idea was not only surprising but also seemed a bit improbable. She also encouraged me to go back to school, saying that this would lead to my getting a teaching job at a small university. She didn't say what I should study, and although I had always dreamed of going back to school, I had no plan and no money to do so. Her words echoed the tarot card reader and I wondered if perhaps she really did know something about my future. Finally, she told me I was going to meet a kind man who didn't like to sit and watch sports. Odd description I thought!

As a practical person, I didn't have an easy time accepting what those first two psychics had to tell me. But, as it turned out, their predictions came true. I did go back to school and completed my Master's degree in leadership. Then I left my hospital job and was hired to teach at Royal Roads, a small university (the same one I had attended for my Master's degree). And I did meet a kind man who rented me a harp and found me a teacher. He rarely watches sports! And as of this writing we have been married for twelve years. I play the harp and we live in a house surrounded by trees.

Now I was once more feeling adrift, and I wondered if talking to a psychic might help. In July of 2015, a few weeks after I learned of Pat's death, I was in Victoria, teaching a summer session at Royal Roads University. My friend Julie, who lived in Victoria, told me about a woman named Debra who was a spiritual medium. I wasn't really sure what that meant but I made an appointment anyway. We talked for an hour, and she told me many things about myself that no one could possibly have known. She touched gently on the pain I'd experienced as a child, my nightmares, my night-time tears. And she offered insight into situations I had encountered in my life. Then she talked about my mother, Phyllis. "She is standing in front of you, telling you how much she loves you," Debra said. "Your mother is still alive, right? This is most unusual. It is very rare to have a live person show up in a session usually reserved for voices from the dead. Your mother's love is very deep." I smiled and nodded. I had no doubt about that. Debra went on to describe my dad, talking about the kind of man he had been and describing his death saying that the ice chips I had slipped into his mouth over the last few days of his life gave him great comfort. She said she could smell roses in his room as he slipped away. I was sitting with him when he died, and I had worn rose-scented perfume for many years. She asked me what happened to the watch that was on his bedside table. I told her that my son had it now. She said, "Your dad is standing right here beside you. Can you feel him?"

"Yes," I said, "I can always feel him."

Toward the end of our session, Debra asked if I had any final questions. I did have one, but I hesitated for a few minutes because I was afraid to ask it. Debra sat quietly, looking at me. Finally I said, "My birth mother died in April. I want to know if it's okay to contact my sisters." I didn't ask her any questions about my birth father. It didn't occur to me to do that, and I am honestly not sure why. Maybe because I was so focused on my sisters. Debra closed her eyes for a moment and then looked up at me, startled, eyes wide open. "Who is Patty?" she asked.

I laughed and said, "My birth mother's name was Pat, and I'm sure no one ever called her Patty. Those sparrow-like eyes would have flashed a warning; never a good thing. You said Pat or you said nothing."

"Oh," Debra said. "I don't hear an actual name very often, in fact almost never. She said Patty so I would know I was talking to a woman. Would you repeat your question?"

"Can I contact my sisters?" I asked again.

Debra looked at me and simply said, "Yes." When she said that, I believed Pat had spoken to her, to me, to us. Just like that, the answer was simply "yes." Instantly, I was furious—all those years, all those wishes, all the stories I had created about what it would be like when Pat told my sisters about me! But the fury subsided. I'd received what I came for—permission to contact the girls.

Debra went on to say that my sisters would have different reactions but they would all be glad to know about me and to know me. She also said that the oldest would feel that a great burden had been lifted.

As I walked back to my car I thought about Pat and the secrets she carried with her all her life. I thought about the weight of those secrets and the image of a rosary appeared (Pat always had a rosary close by). A heavy string with smooth, round beads meant to bring comfort and in that moment, I wondered if her secrets were like the rosary beads—holding them close to her heart gave her solace. Perhaps giving the secrets up would, in her mind, only bring pain. To everyone. I hoped not because it was time to find my sisters.

Chapter Nine
Finding Miji

After my meeting with Debra I dithered, dawdled, and procrastinated. It was exhausting. I remembered doing the same thing every time I got a new piece of information while searching for Pat. And then there was the little matter of everything else going on in my life. I finished my summer teaching session at the end of August. September was spent getting ready for spinal surgery that I had scheduled for October—cleaning cupboards and painting stairwells and walls. I knew I had three months of very restricted movement ahead of me, so I was trying to catch up on all the things I'd left for 'another day.'

Then, after surgery, I was housebound, and suddenly I had all the time in the world to do nothing but think. As my thoughts kept returning to finding my sisters, I knew it was time to move ahead.

Search options had come a long way since the days when I was looking for Pat. Over the last few years, I'd Googled my sisters' names from time to time, but nothing had ever come up. This time I tried the youngest sister first because her name—Miji Campbell—was the most unusual. I knew that her actual given name was Marion Joan, but Pat had told me that she never used it. This time the name popped up immediately. Miji Campbell had just published a book called *Separation Anxiety;* she had a website, and she was on both Facebook and LinkedIn. For years, she wasn't anywhere to be found and now she was everywhere. I learned that she lived in Red Deer, Alberta, but was originally from Calgary, and she was a high school teacher. Based on that information, it seemed that I'd found the right Miji. On her website, she described the book as a memoir, which I downloaded and began to read immediately. In the first few chapters, she described her family, including her mother, her father, and her two sisters: Pat, George, Kim, and Robin.

I knew these people! I had followed their lives for a very long time. I knew things about them that they didn't even know about themselves, but they had no idea I existed. In her book, Miji posed questions about certain aspects of her mother's early life, such as why, in 1952, Pat would have left a perfectly good job in Saskatoon to teach in northern British Columbia. I had the answer to that question as well as many others.

Miji described a delightful, happy, and in her words, "golden" childhood. And then she described where they lived: "Our U-shaped crescent is Kirby Place. Tall green streetlights have little doors in the base for short magic creatures. There are stucco houses trimmed in blue, red or brown. Some have carports. Our house is green with cantaloupe-colored trim. On the front lawn, two slender birch trees are staked with wires to keep them safe from wind. Mugo pines flank the front porch, guarding our castle in the Kingdom of Kingsland." A little later she commented: "If our house was a castle, then our mother was the queen. If our mother was the queen, then we were the royal children: sheltered and slightly spoiled."

At that point, my feelings of shame, rejection, and abandonment all came flooding back, and I had to close the book. It didn't matter that I too had enjoyed a wonderful childhood, that I too was loved and cared for. It only mattered that I was left out of this picture. The familiar ache of being replaced by three new girls had returned.

I did go back to the book but was once again stopped in my tracks as I read the first sentence on the top of page 76:

My own mother had been born out of wedlock, the child of a stenographer named Jane Gordon and an unnamed man 'high up' in politics. She was adopted as an infant by a married couple who had no children...

My mother believed these were her real parents until she discovered, at seventeen, some unfinished adoption papers stowed in a steamer trunk. Shocked and confused she asked her mother, who, flustered and angry, yelled at her for snooping through things that were none of her business.

I was stunned when I read that. Pat was adopted!? She was adopted and she never told me? She knew about the loneliness and sadness of being adopted but she never said anything to me? Why not? Why would she keep that information to herself? Was it the shame of being rejected? Was it because she ended up in the same untenable position—unwed and pregnant— that Jane Gordon, her birthmother, had found herself? Unwed and pregnant. In that moment, I couldn't make sense of this newest piece of Pat's life story. Not for the first time, I felt that she had let me flounder when she could have offered understanding. For thirty years we wrote back and forth, met from time to time, and yet, not once in all those years did she disclose that vital fact that we shared the stigma of being born out of wedlock. As I reread the passage in Miji's book, I was overwhelmed by anger and humiliation—for a moment. Where was her compassion for me? Could she not see that sharing her birth story could help us both? And her refusal to talk to me about my birth father replicated her mother's response. Could she not see how refusing me my birth story hurt me in the same way she was hurt so many years before? Her silence just reconfirmed the validity of my own long-held feelings of shame and rejection. And in the next moment, a rush of compassion for Pat washed over me. To live for over sixty years with such a secret! I reached out to her in my mind and held her close. Over the years, I came to understood why she kept me a secret but in that moment, something unlocked inside of me and I saw her differently. It was as if my heart opened to her in a way I had resisted for so long. She shared my shame and she lived in fear of others finding out about her secret—not just her secret child but her own adoption. I closed the book again.

A few days later, I opened it again. I was grateful that there were no more big surprises about Pat. By the time I finished reading it—twice in fact—I saw Pat and her family with much more clarity. Miji's narrative brought a new perspective to the bits Pat had shared with me in her letters. And it showed once again just how reticent Pat had been to share too much information with me. She walked a such a fine line all the time—not too much information, not too little, just enough to keep me interested. A modern-day Goldilocks, always looking for the elusive balance.

I knew I wanted to contact Miji, but what would be the best way to do that? I could send a message to her website but that felt too impersonal. And what if she had a secretary who read all her email? A note from your 'long lost sister' might get deleted by a diligent helper. No phone number appeared for a Miji Campbell in the Red Deer phone book, and, realistically, would I have picked up the phone and called even if I did have her number? In the end, I decided to write a letter, but there was still one little problem—without a listing in the directory, I didn't have her mailing address either. I turned to Anne, my wonderful and resourceful friend from the days of Mums and Tots, because her family still lived in Red Deer. They had helped me find Pat; maybe they could also help me find Miji. One phone call, two texts, and fifteen minutes later, I had an address. It turned out that Anne's niece was good friends with Miji's son! Once that problem was solved, I wrote the letter and printed it on heavy, cream-colored paper so that it would look important, not something you'd automatically toss in the trash thinking it was junk mail. Many revisions later, I decided to just get on with it and tell her why I was writing:

Dear Miji,

My name is Kim Gunning-Mooney and I live in Vancouver. I happened across your book and that has led me to write you this letter. We have just connected on LinkedIn which is quite weird given what I am about to

write about! You may want to have a cup of tea or a glass
of wine close by as you continue to read...

I have known about you and your sisters since 1985. I
was adopted as a new baby...three months old...in 1952. I
always knew that I was adopted and, as many adoptees, had
a desire to search for my birth parents. And so, in 1984 I
began...long story short...I found my birth mother and she
was Pat, your Mum. I am the reason she went to Fort
Nelson. [I didn't know the name of the place Pat had gone
to when she was pregnant with me, just that she had moved
to northern BC but Miji said in her book that her mother had
gone to Fort Nelson. Her mother told her she went there to
teach.]

Take a breath, have a sip...

I then told her about myself and my family and about
the relationship I had with her mother. When it seemed like
I had said enough, I stopped writing and mailed the letter. It
was October 21, 2015, some thirty years after I sent my first
letter to Pat. And then I immediately began to have doubts,
just as I did after mailing my first letter to Pat. What had I
done? What would Miji say? Would she respond? Maybe
she'd read the letter and decide it was sent by a crazy
person. Maybe it wouldn't even be delivered; it would just
languish in a pile of lost mail. On and on, I tortured myself.

My phone rang eight days later–on October 29. It was
early evening and I was lying on the bed; in the same spot I
had been for days. I saw the name 'Campbell' and for an
instant I thought it was my daughter. Her last name was
Campbell. But then I remembered that only her first name

showed up on my caller ID. Finally, I realized it must be Miji. For a few seconds I simply stared at the phone. Then I tossed it across the bed. I couldn't answer it. What if she were calling to scream at me? Call me a liar? Call me any number of names? Demand to know why I was accusing her mother of such a thing? The memory of Pat's initial anger when she was contacted about me flooded back into my mind. Like in a roulette game, Pat had placed all her chips on one bet—not being discovered. She lost the bet. Now it was my turn. I was betting that my sisters would want to know about me. I wasn't ready for the answer so, I waited. The ringing stopped and the message light flashed. I waited just a little longer, fingers crossed, just like when I was a child sending a prayer to the first star in the night sky. Finally, I listened to the message, and my eyes filled with tears. She said she knew it; she just knew there was a me out there. She hoped I would call her back. It was a beautiful message. A few minutes later, an email arrived.

Hi Kim,

I've been looking at that creamy envelope for the past couple days, thinking, "I'll read that when I have a few moments to appreciate the time someone took to send a letter." I opened it tonight. I opened the wine after my first read and read it again. And again. I phoned and left a message on your cell. I'm absolutely thrilled with this news and there's a part of me that knew this all along. I'm not going to share this with my sisters quite yet, not until I speak with you. (Robin lives in Kelowna and Kim in Calgary.)

Please, let's set up a time to talk on the phone. I'm in the thick of my own teaching term here in Red Deer (you may have mentored some of my colleagues at RRU!) but can make time when you can. I'll be on a quick book tour in Vancouver on Saturday, November 14, but you'll see all that in my e-newsletter I'm working on tonight – if I can just get focused now! ( ) I have a little reception scheduled on the evening of November 14 at Mahony & Sons [a bar in Vancouver] and I think it would be most amazing if you could come!

My head is spinning – and it's not just the wine.
Thank you so much for writing this letter.
Miji

I waited half an hour before calling her back. Sixty-three years as Pat's secret and now the door was open. I was really scared. What was I getting myself into? For one moment, I wondered if being a secret hadn't really been a safe place for me to sit in judgement of Pat for the decision she had made. But in the next moment, I knew that wasn't true.

Thoughts and feelings crashed around inside my head, but then there was quiet, and I picked up the phone. I wanted to meet my sisters.

Miji answered on the first ring. Her voice was filled with excitement and she talked so fast that I was having trouble keeping up with her outpouring of thoughts and questions. She said she was both shocked and relieved by what I had said in my letter. She said that Pat was a secretive person and that she, Miji, had always believed there must have been something in her mother's past she never spoke about. She told me that her mother was a deeply sad woman, but she had always thought the sadness came from the

125

upheaval of Pat's childhood. "You know," said Miji, "finding out she was adopted." Since I had just found it out myself and was still reeling from the fact that Pat had never told me, I didn't have much to say about that. I knew Pat was a secretive person; how could I not? I was perhaps her biggest secret, and I felt her sadness every time we met. I had figured at least some part of that was connected to me, but finding out that she too was adopted added a whole new dimension to her sadness. It seemed as if my picture of Pat was like looking into a kaleidoscope. Every time I thought I was seeing her clearly; a new piece fell into place and the image shifted.

Miji said that when she was doing research for her book, she got a copy of the long version of her birth certificate. The long form contains a space for the number of live births a woman has had, including the one for which the current certificate is issued. Miji's long form certificate indicated that Pat had three live births before Miji when, in fact, Miji believed it should have said two. Kim would be the first birth and Robin the second. As far as Miji knew, her mother had not lost a child so where did the extra live birth come from? She asked her mother about the discrepancy, but Pat had just shrugged it off as a clerical error. She said she had only two live births before Miji, three in total. Miji said she didn't know whether to believe that, but because of her mother's insistence that it was a mistake on the document, she let the matter drop. Miji never forgot about that discrepancy however, and believed that, in spite of what her had mother said, there was perhaps another child out there somewhere. She also admitted to having a very robust imagination and said that she may have been projecting her own hopes for a much more interesting story from her mother than simply, a clerical error!

Our conversation hopscotched all over the place. We talked about our families, our education, our early lives, our middle lives, and then we circled back to Pat. Miji kept saying over and over, "How could she do this? Why did she do this? I don't understand. I was single and pregnant at twenty-nine, just like her." It seemed that Miji had walked the same path as both her mother and her maternal grandmother—unmarried and pregnant—although unlike them, she married the father of her child and they went on to have another. But Pat's response to Miji's pregnancy didn't include her own story. She simply said she would help and support Miji in any way she could. I wondered what Disa, Pat's adoptive mother, would have said about Pat's pregnancy if she'd had the chance.

Finally, Miji said, "I can't go to work tomorrow. I just can't. I have to talk to Kim and Robin. Wow." When we finally hung up after promising to talk again soon, I was exhausted.

I don't remember everything we said that evening but I do remember how kind and welcoming Miji was to me. And I don't know exactly what she said to her sisters when she called them, but I learned that they all had always believed there was a 'me' out there somewhere. In the moment, my existence was a shock, but, at a deeper level, it seemed that a lifetime of questions had been answered. The profound sadness Pat always wore like a cloak now made sense.

Robin called a few days after she found out about me. She said that when Miji told her about my letter, her knees gave way and she found herself on the floor. She said, "I never wanted children. Why would I? I used to think that children made you sad. My mother was always sad, and I thought it must have been our fault." My heart ached. But Robin did have children, two sons, and she had learned that being a mother didn't make her sad. As I listened to her talk, I was reminded that we all make choices in our lives, and whether they are good or bad, the ripples caused by those choices continue to impact our lives for better or worse. How might our lives—Pat's, my sisters', mine—be different today if Pat had trusted the girls with the whole story of her life?

Both Miji and Robin expressed surprise that my name was Kim. When I explained to each of them that their mother had named me and my parents simply chose to keep the name, their surprise turned to shock. I wondered what Kim was thinking! I wanted to contact her, but I was holding back, worried about what she might be feeling after she found out there was another Kim. I waited five weeks, by which time I had already met Miji at her book party. When I finally sent Kim an email, this was her immediate response:

Hi Kim Frankly it's been more of a jaw-dropping giggle than anything (if that's even a physiological possibility). To date, I have been letting Miji be the contact with you since she loves being the social convener and because it has been so thrilling for her to meet you as part of her book's journey.

Both my sons laughed out loud when I told them "The Tale of Two Kims." You have nothing to fear about our reaction to your news. It lifted 60 years of inexplicable burden off my shoulders and 57 years off Robin's.

Cheers, and we'll meet up some time.

I wasn't sure that it was a jaw-dropping giggle, but I did believe Kim when she said that finding out about me had lifted a huge burden from her shoulders, just as Debra, the psychic I had talked to in the summer, had told me it would. I sent her another note at Christmastime, but we didn't actually talk until we met in person in February 2016, three months after I sent my letter to Miji.

I didn't know what to expect from Miji's book event, but I was eager to attend—until I arrived. The moment Chad, and I walked into the room, I stopped dead in my tracks, ready to get out of there before anyone spotted me. Then I felt a gentle hand on the small of my back. I turned, and my husband smiled at me. "It will be okay," he said. "I'm here with you." Just then Miji saw me and waved. I recognized her from the pictures on her book jacket and website. She was taller than I am, with short, fair hair. She was wearing a black sheath dress and a single strand of pearls. She said she recognized me from pictures she'd found on Google posted by Royal Roads University. What did we ever do without Google? As she came towards me, tears pricked my eyes. She hugged me before taking my hand and then she began introducing me to the other guests. She'd obviously told them about me, because everyone seemed to know who I was and why I was there. They all seemed happy to meet me. I was the missing sister, missing no more. It was a most extraordinary moment. Someone put a glass of wine in my hand and I took a grateful sip.

After about an hour of chatting, Miji addressed the group, thanking each person individually for their contributions to her book launch. Finally, she looked directly at me and said that her book had brought unexpected surprises but none so big as my letter. She thanked me for my courage. She said that I had answered many questions for her and her sisters. Then, carefully, she removed the pearl necklace she was wearing and said, "This was my mum's and it belongs to you. You are the oldest sister." Everyone in the room fell silent as she put around my neck. I was not expecting this gesture. Tears rolled down my face. I had no words. Miji hugged me again, and this time the hug lasted a very long time. Then the silence slowly gave way to applause. I still had no words. The need to flee was overpowering, and I stepped out of the room, but only for a few minutes. As with my children so many years ago, I knew that to leave would be wrong. Instead I took a big breath, steadied myself and went back inside. I am never very comfortable in a large social setting and this night was no exception. But it was also an exceptional evening so I did my best, chatting with people, laughing when I thought it seemed appropriate, and generally tried to act normal. At the end of the night I was exhausted and needed to go. Not flee, just go home. In the car, Chad left me to my thoughts and the jumble of feelings that rolled and spun inside me. I touched the pearls that lay on my neck and silently thanked Miji once again for her welcoming gesture. And I thought about Pat, wondering what she would have made of the evening. I wasn't sure she would have been pleased. But I knew one thing for sure—I was very happy I sent my letter to Miji.

Chapter Ten
Meeting Robin and Kim

My letter to Miji had opened the door to a new chapter in my life. Having met her, spoken to Robin on the phone several times, and emailed with Kim, I wondered what would be next.

As it turned out, that was another question Miji answered for me. She thought the four of should get together, and so, in February of 2016, we spent two days at a hotel in Calgary, which was central for all of us.

In the days leading up to that weekend I spend endless hours reliving the two weekends I spent in Calgary with Pat back in the 1980's. All I had to do was close my eyes and I could smell the two different hotel rooms I stayed in. I could taste the glass of wine I had the first night of the very first night in the restaurant. I could see her face, smiling on the first visit, grim on the second. And then, for just a moment, I saw her face on my last visit, smiling once again, a lift of her fingers as she waved goodbye.

To this day, I find it difficult to describe the experience of that weekend with my sisters. When I first heard Miji's proposal, I was scared, exhilarated, overwhelmed—the list goes on. As the date approached, I began to second-guess the whole idea. I wasn't sure I was up to meeting them all at once face-to-face, but since I was the one who had set this whole reunion in motion by writing to Miji in the first place, I felt compelled to follow through. Memories of my first visit with Pat continued to swirl in my mind.

I gathered my thoughts and boarded a plane for the short flight to Calgary. Once I was seated, I looked around and wondered why everyone else was taking this trip. Business men and women making their way to work or home, parents going to see children, children off to see parents—I had a story for every one of them. But I also had a feeling that my reason might win the prize. I had known about my sisters for thirty years. They'd known about me for a couple of months. I couldn't help wondering if we were really ready for this.

When I landed, Miji was sitting on a bench with her back to me. As she turned and saw me, a big smile creased her face. The short fair hair was the same as when we met in Vancouver but she was dressed much more casually in jeans, a fawn colored sweater, and a pair of trendy hiking-meets-Fifth Avenue boots. She explained that Robin would be arriving from Kelowna in a few minutes, so we sat together on the bench and chatted as we waited for her. I had such a clear picture of Robin in my mind that I honestly believed I would recognize her instantly. But, in fact, she looked nothing like I'd imagined. All Pat had told me was that Robin had dark hair—not much to go on! And I had a photo taken the year before that Miji had sent me of the three girls together with Pat. In the picture, Robin looked tall and slim, with an athletic build. In actuality, she was slim for sure, but tiny, like her mother. She had shoulder length dark hair and hazel eyes. She wore black pants and boots, but her jacket was the stand-out feature of the entire wardrobe. It was a beautiful shade of robin's egg blue, the same color her mother wore the day I met her for the first time. It was quilted and snug fitting but it was the color that stood out. Stunning. Robin smiled, said hello, and gave me a hug. Her voice had a sing-song quality that I had become familiar with from talking to her on the phone. Then she and Miji chattered to one another as I tagged along, trying to adjust the image I'd had in my mind to flesh-and-blood woman walking next to me.

Since Kim lived in Calgary, she wouldn't be staying at the hotel, but Miji said she would meet us there. The thought of meeting Kim was still daunting for me. I'd imagined it over and over, and now my imaginings were about to become reality.

Once we'd arrived and checked in, I took the elevator down to Miji and Robin's room and knocked on the door. When it opened, Kim was standing there. I reached out to her and, after a moment's pause, she allowed me to hug her. But she stepped away quickly and moved to a chair on the other side of the room. I perched on the end of a bed and waited to see who would speak first. My memory of that conversation is blurry. We sipped wine and tried to find a topic that was safe for all of us. It felt eerie, overwhelming, particularly because when I looked at Kim, all I could see was her mother. Kim was Pat's double, not only in looks but in mannerisms. I was fascinated. She was shorter than her sisters, with very short silver-grey hair and her eyes were pale, almost an aqua blue. She wore a heavy, dark colored sweater and blue jeans. But her physical appearance quickly became secondary, because her facial expressions and gestures mesmerized me. It was as if I were sitting across from Pat. The way she moved her mouth, the way she twisted in her chair, the way she was constantly tapping her fingers—all mirrored what I had seen in Pat over the years. I wondered what Pat would have thought if she could have seen us all together.

On that first evening, I asked Kim how she felt when Miji told her about me. She said, "It explained so many things to me. I never liked my name, and maybe that was part of why Mum and I never got along." Maybe. But that seemed like an odd reason not to get along with your mother. I decided that perhaps she was as nervous as I was and simply blurted out the first thing that came to her mind. "Well, you can always change your name." I said, jokingly. "You kind of look like a Liz to me." It seemed that my nervousness caused me to say silly things too! Strangely enough, it turned out that her Catholic confirmation name was Elizabeth and she liked that name.

She said she was happy to know about me, but it seemed to me that she wasn't able or maybe willing, to really connect with me yet. I was fascinated by the fact that she was so like her mother, and at the same time, she seemed angry with Pat. I wanted to ask her more questions about her relationship with her mother, but I didn't want to overstep my bounds or push too hard. I wondered if she would ever want to talk to me about her life.

Miji, Robin and I met for breakfast the next morning. Once that was over, they suggested we go to Chinook Place, the shopping center their mother loved to frequent. Pat and I had wandered around there on my first visit so it seemed like a good idea—a kind of pilgrimage if you like. I bought a fancy black purse I didn't need that has turned out to be a lovely memento for me. Kim was meeting us at the hotel in the early afternoon, so once we finished at the mall, we headed back. She arrived with several boxes full of her mother's 'stuff' and began spreading things out on the table. There were photographs of Pat, George, the girls at various ages. There were pictures of summer vacations, concerts, and other family events. There were letters, cards, and awards that Pat had received throughout her teaching career. None of my letters was in any of the boxes. There was nothing that even hinted of my existence except for one photograph of my two children when Shawna was seventeen years old and Matthew was fifteen. I had sent her many pictures over the years, and I wondered why she chose to keep that particular one. It had been sealed inside a blank envelope and no one had bothered to open it until that afternoon. As she looked at the photo, Miji shook her head and asked the question we all were thinking: How could her mother have kept so many secrets for so long? None of us even tried to answer that one.

Then we came across four black and white photos the girls had never seen. Three of them were of a man on his own. In two of the photos he was wearing a white or light-colored shirt and dark pants—standing outside in snow, leaning on a pair of cross-country ski poles. He looked tall with light colored hair and he was smiling. In the third photo, he was leaning against a car, smiling like he was in the first two. In the fourth photo, he was sitting with Pat on the hood of the same car. Pat's hands were resting on her belly. They were leaning into each other, as if completely at ease. He was not George, their father. Could this have been my father? The pictures were black and white so heaven knows if his eyes were brown like my father's eyes were supposed to be. No names on the backs of the pictures, no identification of any kind, leaving us with just lots and lots of maybes and what ifs.

Then suddenly, out of the blue, Miji casually commented that she was surprised Pat had treated me the way she did, considering her own experience of discovering that she was adopted and meeting her own birth mother. Miji clearly assumed that Pat had told me all about this, but, of course, she never did. I only found out about her adoption when I read Miji's book. Kim and Robin were staring at me, waiting for some kind of answer but I had nothing to offer. They too were shocked that Pat hadn't told me about her own adoption. They thought that if their mother had talked to anyone about her own adoption, it would have been me. They wondered, why not? I did too. Once I explained that Pat had never uttered a single word about her adoption to me, Miji retold Pat's birth story to all of us. Pat had been adopted as a baby in 1923. The adoption was never formally completed, but her adoptive parents carried on as if it were—Pat was their daughter as far as they were concerned.

It was a time when babies could be passed over to anyone willing to take them. In this case, Pat had been given to a couple her birth mother knew, and her adoptive parents had moved from Winnipeg to Saskatoon shortly thereafter, so Pat herself didn't even know she was adopted until she was seventeen years old, and happened to come across the incomplete adoption papers.

At that point, Pat traveled to Winnipeg to meet her birth mother, but it was a one-time event. Miji said that Pat's birth mother had given her the basic facts—who her father was, why they didn't marry, and how she had come to be adopted by that particular family but, neither Pat nor her birth mother was interested in continuing the relationship. In fact, Miji said that, until she found out about me, she had always assumed her mother's sadness was the result of her having found out she was adopted. Pat had loved her parents, and so Miji assumed that she must have been very upset to learn that she wasn't their biological child.

As Miji continued telling Pat's story, I became lost in my own thoughts. *Why didn't she tell me? She must have understood how I felt about being adopted, but she kept her own thoughts and feelings to herself, much as she did so many other things in her life.* These were the same questions I had asked myself when I read Miji's book. I still had no answers.

But the more I thought about it, the more I understood how she must have felt when she became pregnant and realized she was repeating her mother's journey. I was pretty sure this was not the life she had imagined for herself, and while I was still angry about the unnecessary pain her need for secrecy had caused us both, I could also feel a deep compassion for her situation. For the moment, however, I tucked my feelings away and focused on staying present in the conversation that was going on around me.

The afternoon passed. There was laughter and disbelief and speculation. The speculation focused on who my father might have been. Each of the three women had her own ideas about what might have happened and who the man might have been. They just couldn't understand why Pat wouldn't tell me. The ease with which they bantered and chattered left me once again feeling like an outsider sitting on the sidelines, watching but not participating in what was going on around me. But I was an outsider, a stranger. I wanted so much to be on the inside, part of their 'sister' world. Instead, I was from Pat's other life, the one before George and these three women, the one that she kept secret. I was relieved when the afternoon finally came to an end. As Kim repacked her boxes, she handed me the Cameron bear I had given Pat ten years before. "You will want this," she said.

We went for dinner later and it was more relaxed than I would have anticipated. The restaurant was Italian, filled with people and very noisy. Our conversation was light. We talked about our children, our work—topics we had touched on before, nothing too deep. And we steered away from discussing Pat. I'm not sure what the others were feeling but for a while, I forgot that I had just recently met these three women. I was having a good time!

When we finished, we headed back to the hotel and once more gathered in Miji and Robin's room to talk. They talked about the sadness that had shrouded their mother. They talked about her secrecy, her relentless refusal to discuss her life before they were born. There was a wistfulness in their voices as they told me their stories. I realized that rejection and abandonment come in many forms, and I was sad for each of us. None of us had known Pat completely, and, because of that, all of us had been left wondering what we'd done wrong. Eventually the conversation wound down. We were spent, and it was time to say good night. Miji, Robin and I agreed to meet for breakfast and Kim said she would join us for lunch. Kim and I left the room together. It was an awkward moment. She was ahead of me but didn't turn to face me when she said goodbye, she lifted her arm into the air and gave a quick wave before disappearing into the elevator.

Robin and I had flights on Saturday afternoon and Miji was driving home. I asked her if we could drive by their family home on the way to meet Kim for lunch. I wanted to see the place to which I had sent mail to for thirty years. Not only was Miji happy to oblige, but she also told me that the people who lived across the street from her parents were still in their home and she was sure they would love to meet me. The woman had been Pat's friend, and Miji had called them when she found out about me. Now she grabbed her phone and started to dial. Robin sat up straight in the back seat and said, "No, Miji, we talked about this. No."

Miji said, "I know but I am doing it anyway." I wasn't sure why Robin was so opposed to the idea, but before I had a chance even to ask, Miji was out of the car. Two elderly people were standing on their snowy front step and waving at her. The whole thing was very awkward. They smiled at me and beckoned us all forward. Miji, Robin and I stepped inside the house, and for a few minutes we stood chatting and pretending that this situation was somehow normal. But it wasn't normal, it was bizarre. Ah, now I understood Robin's reluctance! They said how pleased they were to meet me. Why were they pleased to meet me? None of it was making sense to me. My need to flee was in high gear. After a few more minutes, we said a clumsy goodbye. As the elderly woman hugged me, I saw sadness in her eyes. I wondered if she wished Pat could have confided in her. But I knew Pat couldn't have shared her secret with anyone.

On the plane, my stomach hurt, my head ached, and my eyes burned. The visit had gone well, really well. My three sisters could not have done more to make me feel welcome. And yet it brought up all the same thoughts and questions that had raced through my brain for my entire life—why me?

Once I got home, I thought about everything that had happened since the day I mailed my letter to Miji. I dug around in my mind, sitting with the feelings that came up, taking them out one by one and examining

g them, trying to understand the source for each one. Eventually, I realized I was drowning in self-pity. What a loss! I was missing out on the wonder of what was happening. For thirty years, I had longed to meet my sisters, and now, instead of focusing on that magic, I was sitting around feeling sorry for myself. Did I want to know my sisters? Yes, I did. Those old voices in my head were telling me one story, but I could choose another. It was my decision. So, over the next few months, I played a game with myself that I often played with the students in one of my courses to help them become more self-aware. I would ask them, "What brings you joy? What makes you joyful? What makes you glad?" It's a hard question to answer, because it means you need to think and feel. I turned over each of my feelings and realized that I was tired of feeling ashamed. I was tired of thinking about abandonment and rejection. I was lucky. Meeting my sisters made me glad. They accepted me with kindness and care, without judgement. They were remarkable women, loving and open to the possibility of me. Now it was my turn. It was my chance to step up and get to know them, to become part of their lives if they let me. And to do that I needed to know each of them better.

Chapter Eleven
My Sister's Stories

Not only did I want to know my sisters better; I also wanted to know more about Pat. To see her through their eyes would not only help me know her better but would be a gateway into who they were as well. They had grown up with her. I hadn't. In a way, my search for Pat was continuing. She was gone, but Miji, Robin, and Kim were standing right in front of me. Pat's presence and influence on each of them had been profound, just as her absence had an acute impact on me. Our connection was Pat.

During the weekend in Calgary I searched for ways in which I was like my three sisters and those in which I was different. I looked for ways they were like one another and how they differed. And I looked for their mother in each of them. Physically they didn't look at all like one another, and I didn't think I looked like any of them. Kim and I had looked alike as small children, but I didn't see that resemblance anymore. She looked the most like her mother and had many of her characteristic gestures and expressions. I wanted to dig below appearances, to know them more completely as people. I wanted to know if we had any similarities that connected us all to Pat.

After our initial meeting in Calgary, we stayed in touch by phone and email, but our exchanges were mostly about the events of our daily lives. This was at least partly my fault. I was afraid to ask for more, even though they hadn't given me any reason to doubt their willingness to let me know them better. But I kept thinking, they already had each other; why would they need another sister to complicate their already complicated lives. In the end, I knew that my old story about being unworthy was stopping me.

But when I decided to write this book, I wanted to include their stories and memories of their mother. Although it took me several months to work up the courage to approach them, when asked, they all agreed to share their impressions of Pat and describe their relationship with her.

In my mind this was going to be an orderly, interview-type process, with me asking questions I'd written down beforehand and them providing answers I would tape record—with their permission, of course. In the end, however, it turned out to be something very different. They told me stories and I told them stories. We talked about our childhoods, our teen years, rocky relationships, marriages, and about having children. But we also talked about our mother. As they described her to me, I found myself reviewing my own memories of her as well. They spoke with candor; they didn't hold back. Here is what they said.

Kim

Kim left home at seventeen and went to university in another town. She married young to a man who was much older than her. That marriage ended and eventually she remarried. She had two sons from her second marriage, but that marriage also ended and she is now single. She worked in different capacities over the years before becoming a technical writer for the oil and gas industry. In the last few years she had expanded her work to include web design. By the time we met, she had settled into a peaceful and content life in Calgary.

We all spent many years deconstructing my mother. She was a force of nature that had to be reckoned with. My best time with her was when my kids were born. I was more emotionally available. In that period, I felt safer to be around her, some of the walls had come down. I was less guarded. I was okay to let her come in closer, closer than I had for years or would let her come in subsequent years. It was the best time. I just felt okay to have her around, but let me get my guard up and be cautious, have my emotional fences up. My mother was in her total element; young kids are just her gig she would say. She was a great gran to my kids. Interestingly, as they got a little older, I began to keep them away from her.

The relationship with her was one of walls and guards. This was very much on my side. I am seeing Lucite walls—you can see the person but they can't actually get through the walls. It was very much on my side where the Lucite walls were constructed. The relationship was largely cordial, a non-volatile relationship.

The quality of our relationship overall was about durability. The relationship endured long enough that whatever events, processes, ups and downs, complexities I was dealing with or not dealing with, all played out. I have no feeling or sense of incompleteness. The fact that she was durable, enduring, was probably the thing about the relationship that I can say—we did have a chance. Our relationship endured.

Like the durability, I admired her sheer tenacity. Regardless of what was happening, she kept on going. She was always pleasant—she always had that front.

As Kim talked, I understood what she meant. Pat was like that with me—pleasant. Once we got past the rough edges of our second visit, our relationship was steeped in 'nice.'

I wish for nothing different. Nothing. We had things we were teaching each other. She was teaching me tenacity and I was teaching her that she couldn't run the world her way. She couldn't make me feel something just by wanting me to feel it. She had a survivor's conviction. If she was just determined enough, she would achieve what she had set out to achieve. This can work out very well for choices you have made for yourself. But with your children, "I am the best person to decide what is best for you" doesn't work. She believed that I would come around to her way, to be a certain kind of person that she wanted me to be, that I would feel the way she wanted me to feel. She would think, "But I have been there—I have done all these good things for you—why can't you feel toward me the way I want you to feel? Why don't you love me?" I could make curtains till the cows came home but she wanted more. She wanted an overt kind of love. It had to be overt, with a reminder, never forget I am your mother—I was not an equal.

My experience had been different with my parents. As I grew up, our relationship took on a sense of equality. My parents trusted my judgement, believing that I would make good decisions, come to the right answer even when I felt unsure. I was an adult when I found Pat. Our relationship rested on a mutual desire for connection but I had no need of parenting. She couldn't make the kinds of demands she did with Kim. She had to accept me as I was or not. As I listened to Kim, I wondered if this was hard for Pat and if that was why she exerted such control over what she would tell me.

Dad was a man of subtle signals—those signals said I do love you. But she wanted overt actions, even though she herself was not an overt, emotional person when it mattered. She gave a kind of social performance, but when it really mattered, she was behind walls. She was not an example for us. She accepted affection from others—like a grande dame—*but she wouldn't act in that silly way.*

Outwardly, we behaved as two mature women, but there was tension on my side. People who were close could see it. We couldn't be adult to adult. She was always the mother and I the child.

I just thought she had too much sadness.

She was happy to hear about us and was sucked into our ups and downs. She was an emotional sponge but she didn't have emotional courage. She was happy to help others, listen to the problems of the young teachers who worked with her. She would be on the phone for hours and hours. "Your mother has hung out her shingle again tonight," said Dad. She had a reputation for helping others in times of need. But it never felt like there was a peer-to-peer relationship. I think it was her need to manage the relationships, all relationships. The relationship ended quite quickly if anyone got too close. Mum didn't have friends—she mentored young women. You didn't get to be her friend and you didn't get to mentor her. We daughters were glad to know that happened to other people because it meant it wasn't all our fault.

In her letters, Pat would pose questions and ideas for me to think about when I talked about my various life challenges but she never spoke about what she was struggling with, what inner turmoil if any she might be having. I didn't think about that until Kim spoke but it made perfect sense. Pat was very skilled at keeping me at arm's length too.

She had a very childlike model for living her life. Her father left when she was nine years old and her mother had to work. She became the pseudo-mother to her brother and sister. We could get that being a 'mother' at nine would be hard. Nine-year-old girls know all the answers, never admit they don't know everything. We sorted all that out. But there was something else going on as well. There was a hunger for connection—it was a force in Mum—an unsatisfiable hunger and unhappiness that could only be filled by us girls. That was our job, the job that was expected of us. I took my great giant step back and put up my Lucite walls and said, "You can't ask that of me, Mum. You can't ask me to arbitrarily turn on a feeling." And she would say, "Can't you just pretend?" She believed that maybe if you did that, it would happen one day—you would just get happy, what she defined as happy. It happened for her sometimes—just get on with it and you will get happy. If I didn't seem happy to her she said, "Rake the leaves; when you come back in, you will feel fine. I am a good mother."

Nothing but big drama would get me over my mother's steely determination—all-out screaming, throwing myself, going completely ballistic several times before she would relent. She was very competitive: the reason you do things is to show people you are good. She made me play piano. She never got that I was dying inside. "I am going to make you practice. You will thank me, and when you do well and feel happy, then I will tell you I told you so. You will be smiling and understand this is what you wanted all along." Public humiliation finally got through to her. I quit piano. Who lost more? Intense determination fueled her personality, but there was also that intense hunger. And there was an almost frantic busyness to her. You were either fully enveloped in her world, both emotionally and psychologically, or you had to take a stand to get yourself out of it, get really angry, build up an energy of anger and hatred to propel yourself out of the house. It was all she understood. She didn't actively block my leaving. It all went very quiet toward the end of high school. I was deeply unhappy but I wasn't warring with her. I just left and never came back.

I picked up and refined and perfected those parts of Mum in me that enabled me to keep people at a distance. I managed my outer world really successfully, to my own specification, regardless of what was going on internally, and I achieved what I wanted to achieve. I had that level of determination. She did give us a kind of confidence that we could get out and pretty much do anything. Generally, I have a positive view of life, and all that was down to her. That and her tenacity—those qualities within her were all part of what she demonstrated. I also have her cynicism about men, an absence of belief in the romantic or soft side that you might show in rare, very private moments. I have Mum's survivor skills, mostly because I survived her. She was tough, resilient. She coped. I just couldn't fill her gaps.

We lived in a hermetically sealed universe, a hot-house environment. Mum needed to create her own family, different from the one she grew up in. We all made sense of her need to make a perfect family because of her childhood experiences, but she still flip-flopped: I was a good mother/I was a bad mother, my kids were wonderful/my kids were ingrates. The revealing of emotion came through her body; it torqued. Her physical body was torqued.

In the end, I had the chance to say what I wanted; there was nothing left unsaid. At the end of the day, nothing needed to change. She was stubborn. I am stubborn too. We ended without any leftover business.

Knowing about you had a profound effect on how I felt about me. It was freeing. For years and years, I believed that I was reading her the way I did because of my own negative personality, my need to be not nice, but in truth, my adverse reaction was rooted in something very real. Her emotional outpourings, however they were framed and packaged, were as intense as they felt and, in some cases, as suffocating as they seemed. It was very freeing to get out of the idea that we as kids were kind of mean and kind of made it all up and she was the soul of light. She had some pretty heavy baggage, and we didn't know that, but we sensed it. We hadn't been wrong. If I had known about you earlier, it would have changed my feelings about me, about being the bad person I thought I was. Now I know that all that sadness did have its origins. It doesn't radically alter how I experienced her growing up, but it gives much deeper context to this woman we inherited post 1952.

As my conversation with Kim ended, I was reminded of the destructive power secrets can have on the lives of those we want most to shield. Plenty of 'what ifs?' rattled around in my mind but neither Kim nor I was going to get to answer those questions. Pat crafted a new life after me, locking her secret away, hoping I imagine, that all she needed to do was focus on her newly minted life and the memory of me would fade away. But it seemed that despite her best attempts, the loss and sadness leaked out. Keeping her secret, secret, ended up hurting those Pat loved most.

Robin

Robin studied education at the University of Calgary and then moved to Halifax, Nova Scotia, to complete her Master's degree in education. She taught in Halifax for a number of years and then moved to the Toronto area. She met her husband there and they decided to move west and settle in Kelowna, British Columbia. They have two sons, and Robin continues to work as a Special Needs teacher.

The best years of my relationship with Mum were the last ten years of her life. In the first ten years of my life, she was the mother and I was the child. But during the forty

150

years in between I had to really push back. In the end, she saw me as an adult, but it was still hard for her. I had to control how much time I spent with her. If I spent too long, I reverted to old behaviors—sixteen-year-old behavior. The relationship was best for a couple of hours at a time, and I still feel guilty about that. By the time my second son came along, she couldn't focus on me; she had to look after Dad, and with that came a decrease in her expectations of me.

When I think of my Mum, I have good memories. We had good times when it was just the two of us together, but again, for short periods of time. I needed space to be myself and Mum didn't honor my need for space.

Pat demanded space from me too. She gave only bits of herself away to me, crumbs really. If I pushed too hard for information, she either answered in platitudes or she didn't answer at all. Her fierce refusal to tell me about my father was a testament to her need for privacy. It was interesting to me that she struggled to see that what she needed from everyone, her daughters needed from her.

I admired lots of things about my mum. I admired that she had a career. I respected that. She was born into a cohort of women not many of whom could do that. She did the tried path of marriage and children, but she also managed to find the other, to find her own path, to be independent. I admired that.

She was a contributing citizen. She volunteered, she did her church stuff, totally independent. She trod a new or different pathway. She had friends and people and activities She was at ease in some social situations but she was

151

uncomfortable in others. She would play a role so people would never really know who she was. And, she was very caring.

I just didn't want to be part of her activities and she couldn't understand that really. I admired that she created a life of her own. I just didn't want to be part of it.

I admired that she really liked to have nice clothes and she gave them to herself. It mattered to her. It was important to her; quality was important. She always had two really excellent outfits. I thought it was pretty cool. Not that I loved all the outfits—some were pretty weird. But I didn't have to condone it or hate them. I was not there. Being at a distance meant I didn't have to participate in lots of things.

And I thought she had wisdom. She had lots of people who reached out to her for her wisdom. She had tons of good qualities. I could honor and celebrate her from a distance.

I had to push back when I became a teenager. She was sad when I pushed back, but in the end, it was a gift from my mother. I had to push back to establish my own life; it helped me become who I am. It wasn't easy, but I had to do it. She may have been sad because I didn't ask for help.

I wish she could have celebrated who I was instead of wishing I were different. There was a sense of 'should have been/ought to be.'

Pat's aura of sadness permeated both Kim and Robin's memories of her. It sat quietly between Pat and I as well. But it was only when I looked back, when I re-read letters that I saw it clearly. I was too busy wanting her to acknowledge me to the world that I missed her deep sorrow.

It's easy to think how I am not like her, but there are ways I am like her too. People look to me for advice, insight. It's a quality similar to what I watched in my mum. I learned skills from her; I saw how she was with people. I wouldn't say I was a mentor like she was, but I have similar qualities. In the last days in the hospital before she died, people kept appearing—teachers she had known, helped through divorces and other things. People just kept coming and coming, telling stories of what she had done for them. Goodness gracious, she was a support for a lot of people. I don't have the same number of people, but I think I have the same quality; I think it is in my DNA.

Yes, I thought, it is in my DNA too. It started in my teen years and has continued throughout my life— a knack for helping people navigate through tough times.

I am definitely not like her in several ways. I do not in any way have her zest for vacuuming and cleaning. I try hard to be enthusiastic, but "zestiness for vacuuming and chasing dirt" (that is what my dad called it), I don't have any of that in me. I like it tidy, but she chased dirt with a vengeance and felt really accomplished at the end. I get exhausted. I end up with a sore back and a ton of laundry to do.

I laughed and thought, *ah! I too have a zestiness for vacuuming and chasing dirt."* My family might even go so far as to call it an obsession.

She had to know best, be better, give advice, help people who were upset, but she couldn't be vulnerable, ask for help, or let someone see she was in need. You need to be able to show you aren't perfect, that you don't know everything, be vulnerable. She couldn't do that and her choices isolated her. She had to be perfect. In a way, this need to be perfect was a gift from my mum because it reminds me to appreciate my kids for who they are. It wasn't something she did for me.

She had a sense of humor—sort of the "wisecracking dame" as Kim would say, not a wry sense of humor. Dad's sense of humor was self-deprecating. We all laughed at things he said, but Mum would be hurt or mad even though it wasn't directed toward her. She wasn't as good with subtle humor. And she couldn't make fun of herself. Dad could. He managed to see the absurdity, joking about his "bewildering offspring" (that is what he called us). He could chuckle at things.

She was a good mum. And she believed that being a good mum would bring her happiness, joy—make her feel better. She was determined to be the best. She had pure determination during dark, tough times; she did what she had to do. I think what she had to do in giving you up was a quintessential moment in her life. It informed what happened going forward. What choices did she have? I think how courageous she was to make the decision. And it had long-term effects on how she was with us, particularly with Kim. Maybe she thought she could fix things, get forgiveness for that choice, make up for it in another way.

In an odd way, she got me through my twenties, thirties, forties because I had to push back or pull away, if you will.

154

Her need to hold on made me want to get away and that need helped me become more of myself. The dynamic between us was extremely complex, but she was a great mum.

I was always trying to fix her sadness when I was younger. I began pushing back because I couldn't fix the sadness. I thought it must be me that caused it. Sadness was always there.

We—Kim, Miji, and I—we were stuck. Even after Mum died, we were trying to figure out why she was so sad, why we couldn't make her better, why we were never enough. But when Miji phoned that morning to tell us about you, things started moving again. Everything made perfect sense for me. She had that sadness, it was always there, and knowing about you helped me understand, changed my feelings, shifted how I looked at things.

She had been asked point blank by Miji if there was another child and she said no, but there something that drove her, something we didn't know about. I just didn't know what until Miji called about you.

At this point in our conversation, my mind was spinning. I was trying to be the researcher, listen carefully, ask important questions but to be honest, I felt like I was sinking in quicksand. The sadness Robin saw in her mother (and took responsibility for) linked directly back to me. Pat gave me up and her life moved on but despite everything she did, the grief remained, coloring everything else she did and impacting the daughters who came after me.

Many women went through similar experiences—we all have public, private, and secret parts. I think she liked her secret (who your father was), but she could've shared the information with you. If she didn't want to share it with us, she could still share it with you. You didn't have an agenda. You showed her that you respected her parameters, rules. In that chunk of time that you had your secret relationship, she could have shared information with you. And somehow, she could have told us; we could have handled it. But it would have made her vulnerable; in her mind, she would have been less than perfect in our eyes. But it would have made her real too. She could have received support and understanding from us. I would have wanted you to know who your father was.

At the end, there was a sense of peace about her—a bigger sense of peace. You couldn't deny that bigger things were going on in the last days. There was laughter and ease at night in the hospital.

My memories and feelings about her are different now, but in a good way. I understand more now, I understand where her sadness came from. Life doesn't have to be as hard as she made it for herself. We could have handled it! And she was a good mum.

Life was hard for Pat. Secrets can create a self-imposed prison. She couldn't or wouldn't tell anyone about me. Maybe her push for perfection, for her daughters and herself, was a way to make up for the mistake that was me. None of us would ever know for sure. But it did make me look back on my life and my fixation with being 'good.' She spent a lifetime trying to make up for giving me away and one solution was to create the perfect life. I spent a lifetime trying to be good, to prove to the world that I was worthy in-spite of rejected at birth. What a crazy, mixed up lot we were! I wondered what life would have looked like for everyone if Pat had been able to tell the truth.

Miji

Miji studied English and went on to become a teacher. She found herself pregnant and unmarried at twenty-nine, just like her mum (except, of course, she didn't know that). Unlike her mum, she married her son's father and had a second son three years later. When her first marriage ended, she and her husband shared custody of the boys and she continued to teach. She remarried in 2002. Although Miji was a teacher, she always wanted to write, and so during those turbulent years when her children were young, she began building her writing career while she continued to teach. She went on to publish a number of magazine articles and, in 2015, she published her first book, *Separation Anxiety*. She is currently working on her second book.

My mum and I were kindred spirits. The connection was unconditionally there for me as a child and when I was an adult and had to disconnect. When we were kids, she always had ideas for things to do, interesting things going on. We had a rich play environment—a pretend world with boxes, hopscotch, on the basement floor. Knowing now how difficult it can be to have your own interests when you have kids, I admire how engaged she was with us. She was on top of her house, always working on projects, always in the garden. She was one of those mothers—very organized, busy doing things.

When I was older, I admired her independence. She learned to drive [at age forty]—frightening for us, but it showed her independence. She had a really interesting teaching job. Teachers who taught with Mum had nothing but praise about how she got them through their early years. She was well regarded for the right reasons; so many people looked to her when they were in choppy waters. She was a gentle person. I would see her in action at school, and I was proud of what she was doing with us. As an adult, I admired it so much because I know how much energy it takes to be a good teacher.

She came from a world of work and she embraced it. She was very determined in everything she did. She was not a whiner. How the hell did she get all those Christmas presents wrapped? I admired all the reading she did, all the things she did in the church.

As I grew older, I had to make choices on my own. I had to start to close myself off from her, shield my life from her. I had to have a boundary up. When I became a woman and she was a woman, I was still the child. She always knew best.

When I wanted to write about her life as part of my Master's, I thought it would be a way to create a new relationship with her. I wanted her to be part of this process, to be excited, but she wasn't. She was not forthcoming with details, and things slowly petered out. She was a private person. She grew up in a different era and she didn't want to talk about her past. She said, "Why would I want to go back."

Indeed, I thought, why would she want to go back? She had been teaching when she got the opportunity to change direction, she was on the cusp of an exciting new career in radio. Then she got pregnant with me and everything ruined. Her dream job was over in an instant and she had to find a way to build a new dream. Her memories would have been filled with pain for all she lost. Why ever would she want to rehash those old days?

Being adopted was horrible for her and fascinating for me, but, of course, I realize now that this wasn't the whole story; it was the story she gave me. But her sadness in life was not from being rejected by her birth mother, no no no. It came much later, sometime in 1952. It was about having to give up a baby.

Mum and I liked to be social. When we were both teaching in the Calgary Catholic school system, everyone knew I was her daughter, and people would say to me, "Oh you are just like your mum." We didn't have to be the center of attention, but we were comfortable in groups. We were interested in what other people were doing. And we liked presenting, speaking. She was always trying new things in her teaching—on the edge of new things. I admired that. And we both enjoyed shopping, going for coffee. It was exciting to have Mum to myself. She had her special shop where she liked to go—Miss Country Club. And she also needed her time to regenerate; I need that kind of space too. She could do things, but she needed her quiet space as well.

She was a great guide when I was teaching. The advice she gave was rock solid, absolutely excellent. She used to say, "I've been teaching for a hundred and nine years." I used to get angry at her; it made her sound so old. Now I say it. The whole teaching thing was a place we really, really shared; Mum gave me that real sense of teacher vocation.

But we were different too. I made different life decisions. After I had my first baby, I was going to stay home like Mum.[Pat stopped teaching when she had her children and resumed her career in the late sixties when the girls began school.] *I thought it would be awesome, but I was so freaking bored. I just couldn't be home all the time. I went back to work early. And I got to the point where I knew that teaching was not all I wanted to do. I wanted to be a writer. For Mum, that was interesting, but she was never that person who loved writing. For her it was all about papers and presentations, whereas I wanted to do magazine writing. She was very proud of me when I began to get articles published. She had copies of them on the coffee table, but it was a world that was apart from her.*

When I was thinking about leaving my marriage, Mum knew, and she said, "Stay the course, stay the course; stay in the marriage." It was a big divide with Mum. In a way, I was leaving the womb. I was now going down a road she had no clue about, so she couldn't be ahead of me, coaching me and telling me what to do next. I started to hide things from her then, because she wasn't particularly helpful. She wanted to be close, wanted to be that intimate, and wanted to know about everything that was going on, but it just became intrusive. She needed us to need her. I had to disconnect.

When I moved to Red Deer, I learned I could do it without her, I could get through something on my own. Kim was very supportive during my divorce, and I had good friends, good support that didn't come solely from Mum. I didn't have to rely on Mum for everything. And I wouldn't have ventured out if I took my mum's advice.

I wanted her in my life in a meaningful way without having to become a child again. I finally had to tell her that I wasn't well, that I was struggling with depression. She knew something was going on and she kept asking me if I was okay. Finally, I had to say, "I have been really struggling here but it isn't for you to come in and rescue me." She got it. "I am not going to rescue you. You have people around you. I am not going to rescue you. Trust." She didn't say, "Come move back in with your father and me and we will fix everything." It was a huge, huge relief. I had been sitting on my illness and having to tell Mum felt like I had failed, failed at having character. Good people with good childhoods don't have depression.

I have friends I am not afraid to fall apart in front of, but Mum, she had people, girlfriends, but there was always a part of her that was kept so private. She was a magnet for people who needed her advice, but they wouldn't be able to tell a lot about her. Her strategy was, don't ever let anyone get too close because there was a whole construct that could come tumbling down any moment. Maybe she was close to her God. I don't know. Who would Mum fall apart in front of? No one. Who would she call on a bad day? No one. We as daughters could never be that best friend. She wanted so much for us to tell her everything, but she couldn't do that for us.

In teaching, it really helped when she said, "I was so scared on my first day of school." Just like the information,

"Well, Miji, I was twenty-nine and pregnant" would have been a damn nice thing. But she was very supportive and excited about my baby. She said, "This has worked out very well."

She was sad, a part of her was just torn up. Now I can see it was about the choice she had to make. I think she carried that image of that baby with her "like a stone in your pocket." I am pretty damn sure she carried it with her every day. There was a part of her I could never reach no matter how good or loving or whatever I was as a kid—some part that no one could reach. I think she wondered about that baby every night of her life. What was the retribution going to be? What if that baby didn't have good parents? What if? What if? I'm sure it was a relief to her when you came back into her life. My sense is she never, ever got past that. I think she prayed for you every day. I would see her stretched out on the bed just looking anguished, horrible. Lying there was so tortured looking.

By this point in our conversations, the themes that emerged from both Kim and Robin's conversations were rising in Miji's as well. Sadness, secrecy, a sense of something lost. The picture Miji painted of her mother lying on the bed made me shudder. What was Pat thinking? Feeling? Her sorrow was ever-present but the reason why remained her secret. Once again, I wondered how might life have been different if she had chosen to tell the truth.

I would like to ask her, "Who is Kim's father? Who was this man? Were you ever in love?" She could have given

that information to you. But she did share with you—she
trusted you tremendously. She trusted you.

I feel her. She is around a bit more. I think she is at
peace. I think she took my dog! She and Annie are hanging
out. Hers was a life well lived. I feel nothing but love when
I look at her pictures— just pride and love and gratitude.

Pat's sadness and her fierce protectiveness about herself permeated my conversations with each of my sisters. I was reminded once again that I was so wrapped up in my own story that I missed a key piece of who she was because of the choice she had to make. I saw only Pat's resistance to letting me into her whole world, I didn't see her sorrow.

My sisters gave me everything I asked for and more. They shared their stories of their mother and they shared themselves—who they had become because of their mother's influence. All three spoke about their need to push back against Pat's need to hold them close. They were able to come into their own as individuals only after they left home. I suspect that Pat's desire to do the right thing, be the good mother, put tremendous pressure on each of the girls to be the 'perfect daughter.' And the definition of what a perfect daughter was lived in Pat's mind alone, leaving them to try to figure out how to be the daughters their mother wished for. The constant search for perfection was exhausting for each of them, and peace seemed to come only after they made the break from Pat.

Kim left home as soon as she could, and the physical distance allowed for the emotional distance to grow. Robin followed in her footsteps, travelling to Halifax, which is about as far from Calgary as you can get. Like Kim, miles between them created an emotional distance as well. It took Miji a little longer to break from her mother, but in the end, it was just as clean a break, a physical distance coupled with emotional distance.

That said however, once they began to build their new lives and create families of their own, they could come back to her for short periods of time. For all three, having their own children built a new bridge to Pat. Pat loved her grandchildren! And she even had a picture of my children hidden secreted away in her drawer.

Then, as George became sicker, her focus shifted to caring for him. She had to let the three girls fend for themselves, and they did. They not only survived without her constant attention, they thrived. And, by letting go a little, Pat also gave them the opportunity to give back to her and support her when she needed it. As she aged, she could no longer be the one with all the answers, the one who was right all the time, and this made room for her daughters to take care of her.

Whether Pat liked it or was even aware of it, a shift had occurred. Her daughters were women, her equals, and circumstances forced her to accept their help. As children, each of these three women had tried in her own way to make their mother happy, but none of them ever believed she had succeeded. As adults, they kept trying, albeit differently than when they were kids, and still not knowing if they succeeded. But even though they never understood her sadness, they came to accept Pat for who she was.

Growing from children to adults created a space in their hearts where Pat's possessiveness could be managed. The anger and frustration they each had felt toward her eased, or perhaps mellowed. As Pat aged, their acceptance of her grew, and by the time she died, each of them had made peace with her. Miji's final comment about feeling nothing but love and gratitude for her mother summed up the thoughts of all three. Kim's comment about leaving nothing unsaid was equally telling. They loved her.

And they also helped me understand her better. They helped me to see that her insistence on privacy was simply who she was. I had railed against her need for privacy over the years, but now I understood that I wasn't being singled out. She was like that with everyone. I also had a deep need for privacy. I used to think that I had no great secrets but looking back, I did. I told very few people I was adopted. For a long time, I looked at my need for privacy simply as a desire to keep the world at bay but it was more than that—I didn't like talking about being adopted. It was my big secret.

As I learned more about my sisters, I wondered if they were looking at me to see if I was like their mother. So, I asked them if there were ways I was like her and ways I was different. They said I looked like her, especially my eyes. And, of course, I was small like her! But the physical descriptions soon gave way to deeper similarities, and even though they hadn't known me very long, things stood out. Words like organized popped up. Robin said, "You are very organized in all aspects of your life, like Mum, and I think that you find both satisfaction and security from being organized. Mum was also very organized, and from my perspective, she derived both satisfaction and security in being organized. Mum wrote lists daily and often

165

commented on how great she felt when things were crossed off the list."

Miji's thoughts were similar. "I noticed that you, like Mom, are organized, efficient, with nothing left to the last minute."

They also talked about determination. Robin said, "You are very determined that once you set your mind on something you will make it happen. Mom was also very determined, and once she decided something, there was very little one could do to deter or stop her."

They also touched on mentoring and friendship. Kim said, "The similarity that stands out the most is your capacity for mentoring and friendship." Miji said, "I was struck by how you share certain 'relational' skills and aptitudes for outreach, consulting, mentoring."

And they teased me about my love of ironing. As Robin said, "Mom loved to iron—she loved to 'press."

"Doesn't everyone?" I asked. There was a resounding "No."

Then they described our differences. Kim said, "You're more open and honest in your connections with people. Mum was intensely friendly, always drawing people out, but she never allowed people to draw her out." Miji's comments were similar, "You're not afraid to share your feelings and insecurities. In that way, you are very different from Mum." They said I seemed "more comfortable in my own skin" than their mother, that I had a more balanced approach to life, not so frenetic. And finally, there was a big difference in our approach to humor. Robin summed it up when she said, "You can see the humor, irony, absurdity, and insanity of life in general. Mum had great difficulty with the many different levels of humor. She could laugh, but it was sort of 'outside of herself—scripted somehow.' I asked Robin what she meant by that and she said that it was as if Pat laughed because she thought she should, because it was the right thing to do, not because she thought the moment or the story was actually funny.

The four of us are different in many ways and yet similar because we share a biological mother. And to some degree, we became who we are because of a single decision she made many years before.

As I write this, I am sixty-five years old, and I have finally come to appreciate the fact that, when Pat made the decision to give me away, she really had very few choices and she did what she believed to be best for both of us. Over the years, I said to myself and anyone who asked that yes, I understood why my birth mother made the choice to give me up but really, I don't think I did understand. I didn't really accept the stories I had been told. I didn't want to be the adopted one, ever. I was so tied up in the words rejection and abandonment, so wrapped up in my own shame that I was unable to be understanding. But as Kim, Robin and Miji told me their stories I finally saw how heartbreaking that choice had been for Pat. And I could finally accept that she did indeed, love me. Despite her intense fear of being found out, she answered my first letter and she never stopped writing. And Miji reminded me that Pat trusted, something she didn't do easily. She stayed connected to me and she would never have done that if she didn't trust that I would honour her need for secrecy.

Shortly after Pat and I met for the first time, she began to volunteer with young unwed women who, like her, found themselves pregnant and alone. She volunteered for almost thirty years. She did such amazing work that an award for outstanding service was named in her honour. Her family never knew what prompted her to do this work and she never said. I understood why and now, they do too.

How she chose to live with her choice is a bit trickier. She created a plan that she shared with no one and she believed that, from then on, she had to be perfect, which meant that she couldn't tell anyone about the one mistake she'd made. She never forgave herself. What a hard road she travelled.

There is a poem called *The Dash* (the dash being the hyphen often seen on headstones that connects a birth date and a death date) in which the poet reminds us that life is finite and how we choose to live it fills that space represented by the dash. The ups and downs of life are not always in our control, but we can control how we choose to respond. Pat did what she believed she had to do. And I am grateful that she answered my first letter—that was brave. I believe I am a better person for having known her, and instead of continuing to ask *why*, I will use that energy to focus on making the most of my own life in the dash.

I am not a secret anymore.

Epilogue
Surprise!

"Surprise challenges us to be startled awake, and sometimes shocked to our core.

When we set intention and claim purpose, we often set forth with great certainty.

But a gap always opens between what we think will happen,

and what actually does happen.

This gap is surprise."

Christina Baldwin, *Seven Whispers*

I began to write this book many years before my fingers ever touched a keyboard. I lived with questions about my adoption swirling around in my head all my life. The how and the why of my life—*how* I came to be; *why* I was given away—were but two of at least a thousand questions. Beginning to write was beginning the end of a long journey. What I didn't expect were the surprises I would encounter along the way.

I read many books and articles by other people who were also wrestling with these questions. My life in academia suggested that if you consult the experts you will find the 'right' answers. But through it all—the reading, the researching, and the talking—the answers to my questions remained elusive. I thought they, the experts, would give me what I wanted, but it seemed that I had to find it on my own. A surprise.

So, I wrote this story. I had no idea how to start, so I just began. And as I started to put the pieces together, I struggled to find the words to make the story whole, to tell my tale with integrity, with respect, and most of all, gratitude. There were long dark days intermingled with others that were filled with clarity and purpose. They tumbled over each other, but I learned to trust myself, trust that the words would come. And they did. Surprise.

I found my sisters and I was thrilled. But the surprise wasn't that I found them but that they were *glad* I found them. And they shared themselves with me, opened their hearts to me, told me stories about our mother. They didn't know any more about my birth story than I did, but it didn't matter so much anymore because their acceptance surpassed anything I could have imagined. Their mother was as much an enigma to them as she was to me and we could sit together, shake our heads and wonder who she really was. We could chuckle about her foibles and weep because she was gone. We did it together—that was a surprise.

When I asked other adoptees if I could talk to them about their experiences of being adopted, they didn't even hesitate. They too had walked the path of adoption, searching, wondering, finding or not finding answers to their questions. They opened their hearts, dug around, and answered my questions, even when those questions touched deep wounds. They talked and talked. And they thanked me for listening to their stories—imagine! A surprise.

Along the way, a friend reminded me that my story was not unique, thousands and thousands of children have been and will continue to be adopted. All true. However, what I learned in writing this story, was that it was unique because it was about me. Talking with other adoptees about their experiences gave me words to explain how I felt, and their words also answered some of my questions. Paul said he began his search because, "a piece—a peace—inside of me was missing." And when he found his birth family, he said, "it felt like the hole in my heart was gone." His words echoed my thoughts, the ones that have rolled around inside my head all my life. Hearing someone else say out loud what I had struggled so long to express was a gift, a surprise.

Much has changed with respect to how adoption is handled these days. There is more openness, allowing birth parents to know who received their child and perhaps to have a connection with the child and his or her adoptive family. But no matter what, some things remain the same. A woman gives up her child. A child is given away. And because of that, there will be feelings of shame, rejection, and abandonment. There will always be questions: *Why* and *how* as well as *where* and *who*. *Where* did I come from? *Who* is my clan? As John said, "My journey was to find out where I came from, not to find a new family." And when he found the answer he said, "Now, my work is done." That is true for me. I was never trying to replace my family. I loved my parents and my brothers, but they were only pieces of my picture. Like Paul, finding my birth family eased my heart and, like John, I found out who my people were, at least some of them. Listening and writing and writing and listening. I had what I needed. Surprise.

As I entered the final phase of my work, I had one more hurdle to navigate. When you introduce people into a story and use their real names, you must ask for and receive their permission to do so. My older brother, Verd, died before I began writing so I didn't need his permission. Dan, however, was very much alive. Given that, in sixty-plus years, we had never spoken to each other about being adopted, I was very nervous about opening the conversation. Dan lives in Toronto and I live in Vancouver, so between my fear of confrontation and his fear of flying, there wasn't a chance we would have a face to face conversation. Email was our usual form of communication, and I was happy about that. I sent off an email, telling him what I had been doing, including a few highlights, such as finding my birth mother and sisters. Then I explained that I was writing a book and asked if he would agree to let his name be used. Not the typical email he was used to getting from me. Within a day, he answered.

Haven't you been busy! Good for you! I'm glad this has worked out for you.

I have no problem with you using my name.

I gave a big sigh of relief at that point. Then I read further. He said that he had never done any searching but since I had done it, "Maybe one day" he would do something. One day came very quickly! He sent off a letter asking for his original birth certificate. And now he writes when there is news, like when he found out his birth name and the name of his birth mother. It makes me wonder what it would have been like if we'd been talking to each other all along. But no matter what—surprises.

I didn't realize I was angry with my birth mother but, as I wrote, the anger rose in front of me, often blocking important insights. Then, it began to melt away, forgiveness slipping into its place. And through my sister's stories I learned that my birth mother trusted me. She didn't trust easily. This was a treasured gift I wouldn't know about it if I hadn't written my story. Surprise!

If I imagine an artist's sketch of me it always has gaps, but the lines it does have provide definition, structure, and a sense of wholeness. Writing this story has sharpened the focus of my portrait. The drawing is now more complete. I blew away the cobwebs that swirled around my story and I found my courage. And as my dad told me many years ago, "You are not meant to have all the answers." The gaps that remain, well, as Christina Baldwin said, the gap is surprise. And life embraces surprises. Surprise.

A New Chapter Begins

As I put the final touches on this book for the publisher, I heard from Carla, one of the women I interviewed for my book. She had just found her birth mother using an online genealogy site. She hadn't met her mother yet but now knew who she was and how to find her. Genealogy sites promise to help you find relatives through DNA matching. When an ad for one of these companies popped up on my computer right after I got Carla's email (odd but true!) I wondered if that might be a way to find my father. On a whim, I sent off $79.99 for a DNA kit. A few weeks later the parcel arrived in the mail. I followed their directions, packaged the small cargo up and dropped it into the mailbox.

Six weeks later, I received an email from the company with my DNA breakdown—Irish-Scottish heritage. Nothing very exciting. But even knowing that little bit of information sent me on a trip down Fantasy Lane. What if I found my father? Or at least someone connected to him? A thousand scenarios played out in my mind while I waited to see what happened.

Things did start to get more interesting as my genetic codes began to mix and match with other people's. The first match that popped up for me was from 'Mica 9'. I wrote her a note saying I had received a notification from the genealogy site and we had a genetic connection of some kind. I kept thinking that this technology, coupled with people's obsession with genealogy, just might help me find my father. He was still my missing piece. This technology wasn't available in the earlier years when I first searched for him. Maybe now is the time I thought to myself.

'Mica 9' answered my email and when I read the response, I burst out laughing. It was Miji! The first hit on my code was my sister. We had a good chuckle over that and concluded that at least the process was legitimate. The DNA matching process said we were 'close relatives'. We decided that half-sisters were, indeed, close relatives.

Nothing happened for a couple of weeks and then, another email arrived with a new connection—possible 'first or second cousin' was the designation. What intrigued me about this new hit was there was no connection to Miji. It was just me. Miji and I were linked through our mother, connections without Miji meant connections to my father. The match was a woman from the Ottawa area. I told her I was trying to find my father or his relatives. I had nothing else to offer her, but she was eager to explore our possible connection. She canvased her cousins, but nothing came of that search in the moment and I drifted back into the business of life.

A few weeks later, another connection popped up, a woman from Manitoba. The match said, "first or second cousins". I emailed her and she wrote right back, telling me that she and her mother had done the DNA test and I showed up on both their contact lists. Within a couple of days, her mother appeared on my list of matches. Her name was

Lorie. It got very interesting when Lorie's connection arrived. The numbers suggested that we were "close family or first cousins". This was the same descriptor used for my connection to Miji and the numbers linking us were higher than mine with Miji and I. It was stunning news—it was starting to look like I had found another half-sister. Except, Miji was not on Lorie's list of matches. No Miji, no connection to my mother. There was only one conclusion. We had to be connected through my father. Dare I say—our father?

When I first appeared on Lorie's list of matches as a possible half-sibling, I wasn't shocked. When you are an illegitimate child, you are ready for anything. But it wasn't the same for Lorie. She was surprised and even momentarily pleased that she might have a sister. She was an only child as was her father so having a half-sister had a fleeting appeal. She was convinced that I was probably the result of some indiscretion her father had because he had been a bit of a rogue in his day. But, as we dug into the timeline between her birth and mine, three years later, it seemed almost impossible for her dad to be my father. He wasn't anywhere near Saskatoon when I was conceived. A new possibility presented itself and it was a doozy! Was it possible that her mother and my mother had slept with the same man, three years apart and in different provinces? To think that it had been her mother's indiscretion was too much for Lorie to comprehend —shock set in and our phone call ended abruptly.

I contacted Lorie a few days later to see how she was feeling. I didn't want to lose my connection with her because as difficult as this was for her, I knew that she was the link to my father. We talked about our mothers and similarities between them emerged. They were in their late twenties when we were born. They were well educated and they shared a deep faith, devout Catholics. Not women who would be described as having 'lose morals'. They would not be the ones to sleep with a man outside of the marriage bed. Except, Pat did. And it looked like Lorie's mother might have as well. What made it even more unbelievable for Lorie was her mother was married in 1949 to her dad, had been since 1943. The idea that her mother had an affair was inconceivable to Lorie. I understood her horror at the possibility and yet, here I was —the product of one of those 'impossible' events. I groaned inwardly. This was a huge mess.

I always worried that my relentless search for information about my birth family would cause disruption and potential harm. My sudden appearance in Kim, Robin and Miji's lives was a surprise but gave them new perspective about their mother and knowing Pat's secret answered many questions about the odd behaviour she had exhibited over the years. But it also raised questions about what other secrets she may have kept hidden from them and as compelling as the 'Secret Life of Mother' was for these three women, I wondered if there was also a sense of loss and disquiet.

And here I was again, challenging another woman's long held beliefs about her parents. Even though Lorie was enthusiastic about having a half-sister in those first days, finding out that her mother may have lied to her was devastating. She stopped communicating with me. Caution lights flashed in front of me and I took heed. I reluctantly stopped emailing her. I continue to respect the silence she has imposed.

There is a very, very good chance that my father is dead. He would be over one hundred years old if he was alive and that is highly unlikely. And I may never find his family. But, then again, maybe I will. A little spit in a tiny bottle and I am closer than I have ever been.

So now what? I will keep searching.

Documents

Non-Identifying Information:

BACKGROUND OF SUSAN KIM GUNNING

YOUR MOTHER: Your mother was born in 1923 in Manitoba of Irish racial origin, and the Roman Catholic faith. After senior matriculation, she attended normal school, followed by three years of university. She enjoyed her employment as a school teacher. Her main interests were in writing, radio and dramatic work, including child drama and drama instruction.

The social worker described your mother as a very attractive looking girl, extremely well-groomed, intelligent, and well educated. She had light brown hair, brown eyes, and an olive complexion.

She was reticent in speaking about her family but she did tell the social worker that she was raised in Saskatchewan and had one brother, aged 19, who was in his second year university, and one sister, aged 17, in training as a nurse. It was also learned that her parents had separated, with her mother living in Saskatchewan and her father, somewhere in eastern Canada. No further details were provided.

YOUR FATHER: The information we have about your father was obtained from your mother. He was 40 years old at the time of your birth and of Irish racial origin. He had a doctorate and was a university professor. He was 6 feet tall, with a heavy build, brown hair and eyes, and had a very outgoing personality. His health and that of his family was said to be good. His main interests were sports.

Your father was married but had been separated for several years and was willing to get a divorce in order to marry your mother. However, because of your mother's firm religious beliefs, she did not wish to consider this proposal.

Your mother found it very difficult deciding upon adoption but, not wanting to marry your father and feeling unable to give you sufficient and proper care by herself, finally decided that adoption was the best plan.

Your were born at St. Paul's Hospital in Vancouver and weighed 6 pounds, 15 ounces at birth. It was a full term pregnancy and the delivery was normal. Your mother came to British Columbia and Vancouver for her confinement and it was understood that she planned to leave the province after your adoption placement.

You were placed in your adoption home in December, 1952. In the social worker's final report in January, 1954, it was stated that you were progressing very well, were walking, and seemed very bright, taking a great interest in everything around you.

Your adoption was completed on February 19, 1954.

Baptismal certificate with birth name and adopting parent's name:

Going therefore, teach ye all nations, baptizing them in the name
of the Father, and of the Son, and of the Holy Ghost.
Matt. 28-19

The Holy Sacrament of Baptism
This is to Certify

That _Mary Kim Murphy_

Child of _Patricia Murphy_

and _____

born in _Vancouver_ on _Sep 13_ 19_52_

was Baptized on _September 8th_ 1952 in the Church of

St. Anthonys _Vancouver_

according to the Rite of the Roman Catholic Church

by Rev. _G. Hamilton_

Sponsors were _Mrs Elizabeth Ingram_

and _____

as recorded in the Baptismal Register of this church.

_____ Pastor

St Anthonys Parish

345 West 73 Ave Address

Date _5 November_ Diocese of _Vancouver_
_1984_

adopted by Reginald & phillis
(Susan Kim) Smyth 19th feb 1954

NOTATIONS

180

Information from CN about my grandmother, Disa Murphy, that led me to Pat, finally:

Letters from Pat

March 10, 1985

Dear Kim -

Your letter arrived last
Wednesday and has been
read and re-read numerous
times. The original phone call
was, to say the least, a
shocker. The fragmented emotions
are still in a state of mix-up.
It never ceases to amaze me
how resilient we human beings
are - daily life carries on-even
though the inner workings are
explosively chaotic. Which is
all by way of saying- I need

time to set my reactions
on a course that will have
minimal hurt for all concerned
I feel I can ask this "gift of
time", of you because of your
letter and the sentiments you
expressed.

My family is not aware
of you and I must deal with
this as I think best – with the
givens that exist. Even as I
pen these words I am unsure
of the action I will take.

You spoke of the "years"

of searching and your
reasons for so doing. I
do understand your need to
know and someday we both
will acknowledge your efforts
as worth the results, but
again time is the only
levelling agent. Can we become
friends slowly? Curiosity must
be tempered with understanding
and realization that there are
others who could be hurt and I
have no right to do that if there
are other less painful ways of
dealing with recent developments

I hope you do not find this letter 'hard' or unfeeling. It isn't meant to be - at worst it is the 'facts' for me - at best it is a 'beginning' - I have answered your letter. I need your understanding and patience if it is to continue.

If you can accept my present reactions and wish to write another 'mid-night' release please do.

Sincerely,
Pat Campbell.

Thank you for your reassurances that you were not in search of a family. It is calming to realize that you were blessed with a great and loving family. Although I never really had any doubts. Because of those circumstances so many years ago. I'm afraid explanations - if they ever come to be - would never really be understood by either one of us. It is impossible to go back - yet I find myself wasting time and energy in doing just that - going back. All the anger, hurt and misery have not been put aside - as much as I thought they had been. I have a growing suspicion I have not yet forgiven myself - all other parties yes - but not me. And that fact, my dear is not easy to deal with. So, if there are lights and darks in this correspondence, it is likely that very reason. A second Kim could never really take the place of a first Kim - but she would receive all that two Kims could hope for. Weird it? Bear with me - someday it may all make sense.

Thank you for the picture. I don't share it as yet - may

The card Pat gave me at the end of our first visit in July 1986:

Pictures

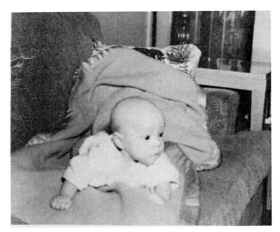

December 21, 1952 – I was three months old;
this was the day I came home.

September 1953 – A family picture of my dad

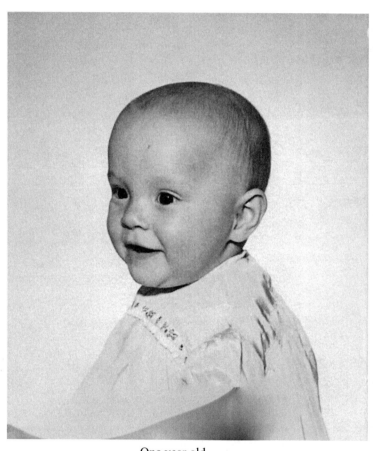

One year old

Sisters:

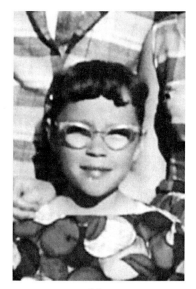

Me

Kim Campbell

Pat and me – different years, same hair!

Pat – 1953

Me – 1969

Sources

Books Quoted

Baldwin, C. (2002). *The seven whispers: Listening to the voice of spirit.* Novato, CA: New World Library

Campbell, M. (2014). *Separation anxiety: A coming of middle age story.* Red Deer, AB: Writinerant Press.

Estés, C.P. (1993). *The gift of story: A wise tale about what is enough.* New York, NY: Ballantine Books.

Lifton, B.J. (1994). *Journey of the adopted self: A quest for wholeness.* New York, NY: Basic Books.

Severson, R.W. (1994). *Adoption: Philosophy and experience.* Dallas, TX: House of Tomorrow Productions.

Sorosky, A.D., Baran, A., & Pannor, R. (2008). *The adoption triangle: Sealed or opened records: How they affect adoptees, birth parents, and adoptive parents.* Las Vegas, NV: Triadoption Publications.

(originally published in hardcover in 1978 by Anchor Press/ Doubleday)

Books for Reference

Johnson, L.B. (2015). *Saving Grace: A story of adoption.* Denver, CO: Outskirts Press.

McMahon, P. (2011). *Becoming Patrick: A memoir.* San Diego, CA: Deep Root Press.

Oren, G. (2016). *Bonded at birth: An adoptee's search for her roots.* USA: Publisher unknown.

Palmer, C. (2016). *An affair with my mother: A story of adoption, secrecy and love.* Ireland: Penguin.

Strauss, J. (2001). *Beneath a tall tree: A story about us.* Claremont, CA: Arete Publishing.

Articles

Child Welfare Information Gateway (2013). *Impact of adoption on adopted persons.* Retrieved from https://www.childwelfare.gov/pubPDFs/f_adimpact.pdf

Is becoming a "people pleaser" common with adoptees? (2012). [Blog post]. Retrieved from
https://adoption.com/forums/thread/380703/is becoming-a-quot-people-pleaser-quot-common-with-adoptees/

Jacobs, W. (2012). Known consequences of separating mother and child at birth: Implications for further study. Retrieved from
http://www.adoptionbirthmothers.com/known consequences-of-separating-mother-and-child-at-birth-implications-for-further-study/

Johnson, L. (2013). *10 things adoptees want you to know.* [Blog post]. Retrieved from
https://www.huffingtonpost.com/lesli johnson/adoption_b_2161590.html

Moore, C. (n.d.). *Adopted voice: If they could turn back time.* Retrieved from Adoptive Families Association of BC.

https://www.bcadoption.com/resources/articles/adopted-voice-if-they-could-turn-back-time

Randolph, B. (2014). *7 core emotional issues in adoption*. Retrieved from http://www.brooke-randolph.com/Blog/7_Core_Emotional_Issues_in_Adoptin

Rummig, V.M. (1996). *Adoption: Trauma that last a life time*. Retrieved from http://www.vsn.org/trauma.html

Schooler, J. (2002). *Why children need to know their adoption story*. Retrieved from https://www.focusonthefamily.com/parenting/adoptiv-families/your-childs-adoption-life-story/why-children-need-to-know-their-adoption-story

Schwartz, A. (2009). *Psychological issues faced by adopted children and adults*. Retrieved from https://www.mentalhelp.net/articles/psychological-issues-faced-by-adopted-children-and-adults/

Silverstein, D.N. & Kaplan, S. (1982). *Lifelong issues in adoption*. Retrieved from http://accordcoalition.org.uk/wp content/uploads/2012/01/Lifelong-Issues-in-Adoption.pdf

Sister Wish (2014). *Shame* [Blog post]. Retrieved from http://www.sisterwish.com/category/home/

Adoption Organizations

www.adoption.ca

www.parentfindersottawa.ca

www.familysearch.org

www.adopted.com